EXPLORING
JEWISH HISTORY

EXPLORING JEWISH HISTORY

by

SHIRLEY STERN

KTAV PUBLISHING HOUSE, INC.

PHOTOGRAPHIC CREDITS

American Jewish Committee, British Museum; Brooklyn Museum; Cairo Museum; Cliche des Musees Nationaux, Paris, France; Cordova Museum, Spain; Department of Antiquities, Jerusalem, Israel; Hebrew Immigrant Aid Society; Hebrew Union College; Jewish Museum, New York; Jewish Theological Seminary, New York; Library of Congress; Metropolitan Museum of Art; Morgan Library; Oriental Institute, University of Chicago; Palphot, Israel; Staatliche Museen, Berlin; Toledo Museum, Spain; University Museum, The, University of Pennsylvania; YIVO, Yiddish Institute for Jewish Research; Zionist Archives, New York.

Library of Congress Cataloging in Publication Data

Stern, Shirley.
  Exploring Jewish history.

  Includes index.
  SUMMARY: A history of the Jewish people from Biblical times to the present.
  1. Jews—History—Juvenile literature. [1. Jews—History] I. Title.
DS118.S8   909'.04'924   78-32142
ISBN 0-87068-651-8

TABLE OF CONTENTS

**To My Mother
Bessie Gartenstein
in loving memory**

UNIT I

WE LEARN ABOUT THE PAST

Have you ever wondered about long ago? How did people live? What did they eat? What clothes did they wear? How did they earn their living? What did they worry about? What did they wonder about?

It is easy to learn about times not so long ago. You can ask your parents. They can tell you what it was like when they were small. Or you may be able to ask your grandparents.

But whom do you ask if you want to know about hundreds of years ago, or thousands of years ago. Often the information you want can be found only in history books. But most history books were written nowadays, not long ago. How do the people who write history books learn about the past?

People who write history books are called historians. In this unit you will read about some of the ways historians learn about the past. You will also understand how historians of the future will be able to learn about our own time, when it has become the "long, long ago" of a future age.

chapter 1

We Read About the Jewish Past

Long before people learned how to keep written records, they had many of the same needs that we have today. They had to eat and take care of their children. They had to defend their homes and help the sick. They used many objects in their everyday living—dishes and utensils for eating, weapons for defense, altars for worship. We call these objects artifacts. When artifacts are found they tell us a great deal about how people lived.

Some scientists make a special study of artifacts of long ago. They spend much of their time digging in far-off lands. They are looking for artifacts that can tell us about how people lived. These scientists are called archaeologists. The work they do is both interesting and useful. Perhaps some day you will want to be an archaeologist and dig up new information about the past.

This stone seal belongs to the period of the Judean king Jeroboam. It was found at Meggido, Israel. The line above the lion reads: "Shema." The line underneath reads: "Seal of Jeroboam."

This inscribed clay cylinder tells a story about King Cyrus of Persia. It describes how Cyrus captured many lands and how these people are bringing him many valuable gifts.

Written Records of the Past

Sometimes there are written records from long ago. They can tell us even more than artifacts do. Although people did not set out to keep records for future historians, some of the things they left behind can be very helpful. Here are some records that have helped us understand the past: A code of laws carved by an ancient leader on stone tablets. A story about religious practices written on a parchment scroll. These things can tell us a great deal about how people lived in the past.

History is really the current events of some by-gone age! Letters people sent to each other, diaries of wars, and even business records all become historical records when they are found by future generations. Many years from now our newspapers and magazines will be helpful. Our books and diaries will be useful. They will teach future generations the history of our own time. Just as history is the current events of the past, so are current events the history of the future.

chapter 2

We Learn From the Bible and the Talmud

On July 20, 1969 an amazing thing happened. Two American astronauts, Neil Armstrong and Edwin Aldrin, set foot on the moon. Before leaving the moon they left a plaque. On the plaque were written messages from the heads of countries all over the world. It was a written record of a wonderful deed. People far in the future will be able to read this plaque. They will be reminded of this heroic feat, and the walk on the moon will not be forgotten.

Long ago people learned to communicate by writing. And since that time they have left written records of their deeds. Today boys and girls often keep diaries to express their innermost thoughts. Captains of ships and airplanes keep logs that record all the important facts about their trips. Great men and women write their memoirs to tell about their important decisions and experiences. Clubs and organizations keep minutes of their meetings. Presidents keep a written record of their years in office. These records are carefully stored in presidential libraries.

Today's records will help future historians understand the twentieth century. In order for us to understand the history of the Jewish people in ancient times, we must "discover" some of the written records left by Jews of long ago. Are there such records? Can we find them? Will they tell us anything about the ancestors of the Jewish people? You are about to take a trip through time. You will explore some of the writings of the ancient Jews. You will see whether we can answer these questions.

This stele (monument) was erected in honor of King Mesha of Moab. The language is Moabite. The inscription tells how Mesha won his freedom from the Israelites led by King Omri.

The Bible

The ancient Hebrews often told each other stories about their God and his wonderful and miraculous deeds. The stories were not in writing. They were passed by word of mouth from generation to generation. Each new generation added its own religious beliefs and something about its own history. Later these stories were written down. Today they come down to us in the Bible.

Other religious groups also told stories about their gods, and some of these stories have also been preserved. But the Bible is a very special record. It tells about the religious beliefs of the Jewish people. It also helps us to know what is right. The stories in the Bible teach many lessons for our own time. For example, the story of the creation of Adam and Eve tells us that the ancient Hebrews believed that all people are descendants of one mother and father. This means that all men are brothers, no matter what their color or which country they live in. This is a good lesson to remember. Perhaps you can think of other Bible stories. What do they tell us about the beliefs of the forefathers of the Jewish people? How can they help us to guide our own lives?

The Bible also contains historical records. You read in the Bible about kings and great battles. You read about a king who built a Temple to glorify God. You are surprised at the just and kind laws of an ancient day. You also read about wicked kings. You read about selfish people who thought only of themselves. Much of the early history of the Jewish people is found in the Bible. We are grateful to those who preserved these writings for us. We can learn about the past of the Jewish people.

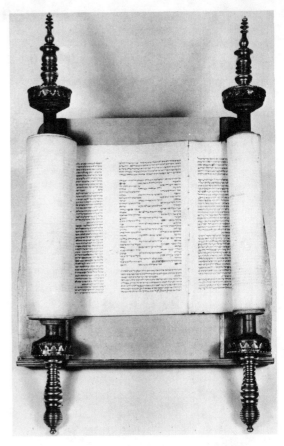

This is a Torah scroll. It is made of parchment and is written by hand. The Torah contains the first five books of the Bible.

The Talmud

The Bible is one of the most valuable historical records. It also is one of the most important religious books. But for the Jews it is not the only one. There are many other Jewish religious books. They all help us to tell the story of the Jewish people. Among the most important is the Talmud.

The Talmud is like an encyclopedia. It contains nearly six thousand pages. It is the work of over two thousand scholars. It covers a thousand years of Jewish history. It contains all of the Jewish laws of that time. It also explains the laws and tells why they are important.

But there is more in the Talmud than just the laws. It is a very human document. There are stories about great scholars. There are fables that illustrate moral lessons. There are also observations on everyday life. And there are records of historical events and descriptions of the customs of the people. It is truly an amazing work. It tells us a great deal about the Jews of that time.

This is a page from the Talmud. The Talmud passage is the large type in the center of the page. To the left and right are commentaries (explanations) of the text.

chapter 3

The Cairo Genizah and the Dead Sea Scrolls

In the last chapter you read about the Bible and the Talmud. They are two of our most important books. They have been carefully preserved down through the ages. They tell us many things about the Jews of long ago.

Some ancient Jewish books were lost and forgotten. If a lost book is found, it is an occasion of great rejoicing for historians and scholars. From time to time such discoveries are made. They add greatly to our knowledge about ancient times.

At the end of the nineteenth century there was a discovery. Rabbi Solomon Schechter was a wise and learned scholar. He made his great discovery in a genizah in Cairo, Egypt. The word *genizah* means "hiding." A genizah is a storehouse for old books. Jews have always loved books and learning. They never threw away old or torn books that had God's name written in them. So the custom grew up of burying such books. Sometimes they were put in a special storage place. Even in our time old religious books and Torah scrolls are buried.

Rabbi Schechter loved to study old books. He hoped that someday he would find a book that had been lost and forgotten. This would be one of his contributions to Jewish knowledge. One day

Rabbi Solomon Schechter

he learned about a genizah in a very old synagogue in Cairo. He decided to go there. He wanted to see what treasures he could find. The genizah was filled with crumbled, dusty books, scrolls, and papers. Among them was an ancient work of wisdom by Ben Sirach. The Talmud spoke of this book. But it had been lost for many hundreds of years.

Rabbi Schechter was very excited and happy about his find. For many months he worked putting the book back together. The book was in many old and worn fragments. It was like fitting the pieces of a jigsaw puzzle together. Finally his work was finished. The book of Ben Sirach could be studied by scholars and historians. Rabbi Schechter spent many more months looking over other old and worn books. The genizah was dingy, dusty, and unpleasant. But Rabbi Schechter didn't mind. He knew that the work he was doing would add to our storehouse of knowledge about the Jewish people of long ago.

The Dead Sea Scrolls

Another important discovery was made in 1947. It happened in a valley known as the Wadi Qumran, near the Dead Sea. The story of this find sounds like an adventure story, but it is a true story.

One day two Arab boys were watching their small flock of goats. They were grazing in the valley. Suddenly they noticed that one of the goats was missing. They started to search for the missing goat. They searched for many hours. One boy spotted a dark cave under a cliff. "Perhaps our goat has

The Dead Sea Scrolls are the oldest Hebrew manuscripts in existence. They are housed in the Shrine of the Book, in the Israel Museum, Jerusalem. The Scroll of Isaiah is displayed fully opened around a drum.

wandered into this cave," they thought. Carefully they entered the cave. But they didn't find the goat. Disgustedly, one of the boys picked up a stone and threw it against the wall of the cave. The stone didn't bounce off the wall. Instead there was the sound of something being broken.

The boys left the cave. They continued searching for their goat. But they couldn't forget the sound of something being broken. The next day they went back. On the floor of the cave they found eight huge jars. They opened them. They had hoped to find a treasure. But all they found were some old parchment and copper scrolls. Little did they know that

One of the Dead Sea Scrolls known as the Habakkuk Commentary. Habakkuk is a book of the Bible.

they had actually found a treasure. Their find was more valuable than gold, silver, or diamonds.

This discovery came to be known as the Dead Sea Scrolls. The scrolls told many new things about the forefathers of the Jewish people. Until the discovery of the scrolls, the oldest copy of the Bible in Hebrew was dated about the year 1000. These scrolls are much, much older. Two of the scrolls were copies of the Book of Isaiah.

Ancient jars found in caves in Qumran, containing some of the famous Dead Sea Scrolls. These scrolls may have been written by a sect of Essenes living under Roman rule.

chapter 4

Archaeological Discoveries: King Solomon's Mines and Masada

Nelson Glueck

How would you like to be a detective? How would you like to solve mysteries? You could carry a magnifying glass. You could look in hidden places for clues. You could learn secrets that nobody else knew!

In this chapter you will read about detectives of a very special kind. These detectives are called archaeologists. They hunt for clues from the past. Their work is adventurous and exciting. The secrets they learn are the secrets of long ago.

Nelson Glueck and King Solomon's Mines

Dr. Nelson Glueck was a rabbi. He was a well-known Bible scholar. He was also the president of the Hebrew Union College-Jewish Institute of Religion where Reform rabbis are trained. But these were not the things that made him most famous. Dr. Glueck was one of the most outstanding archaeologists of our times. He was best known as a detective of the past.

Dr. Glueck decided to try to find the lost copper mines of King Solomon. It was known that Solomon's craftsmen used copper, but no trace of the copper mines had ever been found. Dr. Glueck decided to use his knowledge of the Bible. He used certain Biblical verses as clues. He searched until he found the long-lost mines. The Bible had led him to the mines. He was very pleased to make this discovery.

Dr. Glueck continued his exploring. He still used the Bible as his guide. He found the ancient city of Ezion-Geber on the Gulf of Aqaba near Eilat. It was here that the copper from King Solomon's mines had been refined and made ready for use.

On the same site where the ancient refinery once stood, there is now a modern refinery. It produces copper for the modern State of Israel. The copper ore that is refined there comes from the

An aerial view of the ruins of Ezion-Geber. King Solomon's copper smelter was located in this city.

17

These are some of the items found in Masada. Can you identify these items?

same mines used by King Solomon. So, you see, archaeologists help us to learn about the past. And sometimes they make discoveries that are very important.

Yigael Yadin and Masada

Another famous archaeologist is Professor Yigael Yadin. This detective of the past has made many important discoveries. His most famous one is Masada.

Masada was a fortress situated high above the Dead Sea in Judea. Today Judea is called Israel. About nineteen hundred years ago, in the year 70 C.E., a powerful Roman army conquered Jerusalem. The Romans destroyed the Temple. Then they tried to conquer Masada.

There were 960 Jewish men, women, and children at Masada. They were determined not to be captured. They fought long and hard against the Roman armies. When they saw that they could no longer hold out, they decided to kill themselves rather than surrender. And so they perished, all 960 of them. They died as free people rather than become Roman slaves.

Professor Yadin went up to Masada. He found many treasures that helped to tell the full story of that heroic deed. He and his assistants found scrolls written in Hebrew, Aramaic, and Greek. They found clothing and jewelry. And they found dried food and eating utensils, coins and combs. They also found some objects that brought tears to their eyes. Among the debris there were some children's toys and a tiny gold ring worn by a baby.

Masada, this fortress high on a rock near the Dead Sea, was the last Jewish stronghold to fall to the Roman conquerors following the destruction of the Temple.

UNIT II

WE GO BACK INTO HISTORY

In the last unit you read about some of the ways we learn about the past. You read about how we use written records. You also read about how the discoveries of archaeologists tell us of the history of the Jewish people. In this and following units, you will explore some of the information that has been gained from these sources.

You will begin the fascinating true story of the Jewish people. It is a story that goes back over four thousand years. But it is a story that does not end. It is still continuing in our own time. Perhaps someday in the future, other children will read about you and your times in *their* study of Jewish history.

chapter 5

In the Desert

To learn about the earliest Jews you must go far back into history. About four thousand years ago the forefathers of the Jewish people were shepherds called Hebrews. They lived in and around the area known as the Fertile Crescent, a fertile region surrounded by barren deserts. They traveled from place to place to find water for their flocks.

The ancient Hebrews had to protect themselves. The desert was unfriendly. There were wild animals and hostile neighbors. The early Hebrews lived together in large family groups called clans or tribes. At the head of each clan was the patriarch. The patriarch was the old man of the tribe. His word was law. His decisions were final.

Many of the Bible stories tell about the special love that the patriarchs had for God. They believed that God had selected them to be leaders of their people.

The three patriarchs of the Hebrew people are Abraham, Isaac and Jacob. This is a map of the Fertile Crescent. The map shows you some of the places where the patriarchs lived.

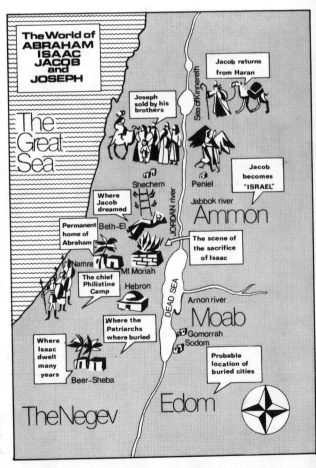

The World of ABRAHAM ISAAC JACOB and JOSEPH

The Great Sea

Jacob returns from Haran

Joseph sold by his brothers

Sea of Kinnereth

Shechem

Peniel

Jacob becomes "ISRAEL"

Jabbok river

Ammon

Where Jacob dreamed

JORDAN river

Permanent home of Abraham

Beth-El

The scene of the sacrifice of Isaac

Namre

Mt Moriah

The chief Philistine Camp

Hebron

DEAD SEA

Arnon river

Moab

Where the Patriarchs where buried

Gomorrah

Sodom

Where Isaac dwelt many years

Probable location of buried cities

Beer-Sheba

The Negev

Edom

One of the Bible stories tells how the patriarch Abraham was chosen by God. God told Abraham to go from the land of his birth to a new land. There he would become the leader of a great nation. The land would belong to his descendants forever. Abraham left his family and friends and went to the land God showed him. On the way he had many adventures, but God always helped him and he settled safely in the new land, Canaan, which we now call Israel.

Another story tells how God tried to test Abraham. One day God called Abraham. He asked Abraham to take his son Isaac and give him up to God. This was called a sacrifice. In those days people showed their love for their gods by sacrificing, or giving up, things they loved to the gods. Abraham was very sad. He loved his son very much. But he did not hesitate. He took his son Isaac to the top of a mountain. There he got ready to sacrifice him. But God did not really want Isaac. He just wanted to test Abraham's love. At the last minute God stopped Abraham from sacrificing Isaac.

Another Bible story tells about Isaac when he grew up. He was ready to get married, but he wanted to marry a girl from his own people. They lived in a faraway land. So Abraham sent his trusted servant Eliezer to find a wife for Isaac. Eliezer went. But he did not know who would be a good wife for Isaac. "God will give me a sign," he said. Soon he reached a well. A group of girls stood near the well. Eliezer said, "Please give me a drink of water. I am very thirsty." One of the girls was Rebekah. She said, "I will give you a drink, I will also give your camels a drink." Eliezer thought, "She is very kind. She will be a good wife for Isaac."

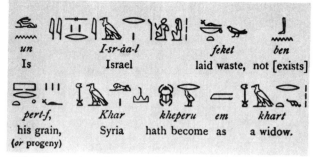

un	I-sr-àa-l	feket	ben
Is	Israel	laid waste, not [exists]
pert-f,	Khar	kheperu	em	khart
his grain, (or progeny)	Syria	hath become	as	a widow.

This is an inscription on an ancient Egyptian monument. It tells about the Egyptian king Merneptah who defeated Israel.

These are just a few of the stories in the Bible. There are many more. They help to tell us something about our ancestors. From them we learn what life was like for the early Jews in the desert. We learn what our ancestors believed about God. We also learn how the patriarch Jacob, the son of Isaac and the grandson of Abraham, had his name changed to Israel. Because of this name change, the ancient Hebrews came to be called Israelites, or the children of Israel.

The Hebrews in Egypt

Life was hard in those days. There was always war among the tribes for the few places where water could be found. Tribes were always stealing from each other. Sometimes they would murder their enemies or make slaves of their

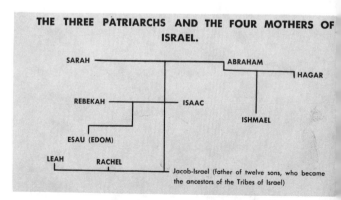

THE THREE PATRIARCHS AND THE FOUR MOTHERS OF ISRAEL.

SARAH — ABRAHAM — HAGAR

REBEKAH — ISAAC — ISHMAEL

ESAU (EDOM)

LEAH   RACHEL

Jacob-Israel (father of twelve sons, who became the ancestors of the Tribes of Israel)

enemies. To make matters worse, there were occasional famines. All the springs would dry up. The sheep would begin to die from lack of food and water.

During one of these famines, in the time of Jacob, the Israelite shepherds wandered to Egypt, where food was plentiful. There they lived in peace for many years. One of Jacob's sons, Joseph, became very important in the Egyptian government.

There were powerful kings, called Pharaohs, in Egypt. The Pharaohs liked to have palaces and monuments built for themselves. They needed laborers. One day soldiers marched into the Hebrew settlement. The Jews were all enslaved.

Moses and Freedom

For many years the Israelites were slaves in Egypt. It was a sad life. They were forced to work hard. They built pyramids and cities. Cruel taskmasters watched over them. They made sure that each slave did his full quota of work. Those who were sick and old had to work as hard as the young and strong.

The Hebrew slaves longed for freedom. If only they could escape. They wanted to live the free life once more.

The Pharaohs of Egypt left many monuments. They built temples, monuments, pyramids, and statues of themselves and their gods. This is a gigantic statue of a Pharaoh. It is about 40 feet tall and weighs many tons.

But they had been slaves for too long. They were broken in spirit as well as in body. There was no one to stand up for them.

The Pharaoh ordered the Hebrew mothers to kill their baby boys. One mother decided to save her newborn son. She put the infant into a basket and floated it down the river Nile. Pharaoh's daughter found the baby and raised it as her own. She named the baby Moses. He was raised in the palace of Pharaoh and became an Egyptian prince.

When Moses grew up, he saw the cruel way the Israelites were treated. He was very sad and angry that his people were slaves. He went to Pharaoh and said, "Let my people go." But Pharaoh refused. The Hebrews were very useful to him as slaves. He would not let them go free. The Bible tells a very dramatic story of how the Israelites were finally freed.

According to the Bible story, when Pharaoh refused to free the slaves, God made terrible things happen to the Egyptians. The water turned to blood. The sky suddenly became dark in the middle of the day. People and animals became sick. Finally, all first-born Egyptian children died. In all, ten terrible catastrophes happened in Egypt. They were called the Ten Plagues.

At last, the Bible story continues, Pharaoh allowed the Israelites to leave Egypt. But then he changed his mind. He sent his army to bring them back. But most of the Egyptians soldiers were drowned in the Sea of Reeds (sometimes called the Red Sea). The Israelites escaped.

Jews retell this wonderful story every spring during the feast of Pesach, or Passover.

The Ten Commandments

After leaving Egypt, the Israelites wandered for many years in the Sinai Peninsula and the barren Negev Desert. They hoped someday to settle in the fertile land of Canaan, which, according to their tradition, had once belonged to them.

In the desert the Israelites developed a new code of laws by which to live. The ten most important of these laws were called the Ten Commandments. One of these laws stated that killing was wrong;

Two paintings discovered on the walls of Egyptian tombs. The scene below shows slaves pressing grapes and making wine. The scene at the left shows slaves taking care of cattle. Notice the slave being beaten by an overseer.

another forbade stealing. Other laws commanded them to respect their parents and to rest from their work one day a week on the Sabbath.

This new code of laws was very important to the Israelites. They believed that the Ten Commandments had come directly from God and had been given to Moses on Mount Sinai.

The people placed the stone tablets bearing the great laws into the Ark of the Covenant. Wherever the Israelites went, the Ark of the Covenant went with them. The priests carried it on their shoulders. These great laws have come down to us in the Torah. They are the foundation of Judaism even in our own time.

The Ark in the Land of the Philistines. **Copy from the fresco in the synagogue at Dura-Europos, 3rd century C.E.**

Yale University Art Gallery

THE TEN COMMANDMENTS

1. I am the Lord, your God.
2. You shall have no other gods before Me.
3. You shall not take the name of the Lord in vain.
4. Remember the Sabbath to keep it holy.
5. Honor your father and your mother.
6. You shall not kill.
7. You shall not be unfaithful to wife or husband.
8. You shall not steal.
9. You shall not bear false witness.
10. You shall not desire what is your neighbor's.

A wood engraving of the Ten Commandments.

chapter 6

Farmers in Canaan

The Israelites left Egypt. For many years they wandered in the desert. They lived as nomads in the wilderness. But they did not forget their dream of a land of their own, a land where they could settle down in peace and plenty. They planned to invade the fertile area called Canaan. There they would make their permanent home.

Moses was the leader of the Israelites. He wanted to march right into Canaan, but the Israelites were afraid. Moses decided to wait for forty years. He waited until the older generation died out. A new generation was born in the desert and raised in freedom. The brave soldiers of the new generation would wage war against the inhabitants of Canaan and capture their homeland.

A photograph of Mount Sinai. It was on top of this mountain that Moses received the Ten Commandments.

This mound contains some of the remains of the ancient city of Jericho. Much excavating is being done at the site.

Joshua Conquers Canaan

Many years passed. The older generation was no more. Even Moses had died.

Joshua was now the Israelite leader. He sent spies into Canaan. The spies returned with good reports of its fertility. It was a "land flowing with milk and honey." Here they could raise crops and prosper. Here the soil was fertile and water was plentiful. This was indeed the place where the Israelites wanted to settle.

The Israelites made plans to conquer the cities of Canaan. Joshua and his warriors marched against such cities as Jericho and Hazor. They destroyed homes and fortresses. Perhaps you remember the dramatic story of Joshua and the walls of Jericho? It is told in the Bible. The mighty walls of Jericho crumbled when the Israelites attacked. You may want to read the story again now that you understand something about the history of that time. There were many other great battles. The Israelites were victorious. When they had conquered enough territory, they divided the land of Canaan among the twelve

Israelite tribes—Reuben, Simeon, Judah, Naphtali, Gad, Asher, Issachar, Zebulun, Dan, Levi, Benjamin . . . Manasseh and Ephraim who shared Joseph's portion.

The Israelites made their homes in Canaan. They lived side by side with their Canaanite neighbors. They learned from them how to raise crops and become good farmers.

The Israelites Become Farmers

The Israelites settled into their new lives. They became better farmers. Even their religious life reflected their new occupation. So important was their new way of life to them that their three most important religious holidays were harvest festivals. They celebrated these festivals in ways that we would find strange today. But it was the way other farming people celebrated in those days. They sacrificed animals and crops. They sang songs of thanksgiving. They danced special ritual dances.

The Israelites celebrated three holidays. The beginning of the grain harvest was the first one. The second was the end of the grain harvest. And the third was the fruit harvest. These holidays are called Passover, Shavuoth, and Succoth. Jews celebrate them to this day. But today the celebrations are different.

The Judges

The Israelites lived peacefully with some of their Canaanite neighbors. But for the most part their lives were not peaceful. They had enemies within Canaan. They also had enemies in the surrounding areas. Hostile tribes were always attacking. War was a frequent part of their lives.

The Israelites themselves were not united. Different tribes lived in different

A limestone carving written in old Hebrew script. It was found at Gezer, Israel, in 1908. The text lists the yearly types of harvest in ancient Israel.

areas. They had very little to do with one another. Soon they realized that this would not do. In order to protect themselves, they would have to band together. They would have to help each other in periods of great danger.

The Israelites did not have a king or central government. In times of trouble, a temporary leader would arise. These leaders would take command until the need was over. They were called judges. However, judge is a misleading name. They were really great military leaders.

Both men and women served as judges. Deborah, a judge and prophetess, defeated the Canaanites who attacked the Israelites. Some interesting stories about the judges are told in the Bible. Perhaps you will want to read some of them. You will find the ones about Deborah, Samson, and Gideon very exciting.

chapter 7

A Jewish Kingdom

In the last chapter you read about the Israelite tribes. They had to band together in times of trouble and danger. You read about military leaders called judges. They would take command until the enemy was defeated and the danger was over.

This continued for many years. But as time passed the enemies of the Israelites became stronger. Their attacks were more frequent. The Israelites knew that they would have to form a more permanent union of tribes. If they didn't, the land they loved would be taken away from them. They would have to become a nation at last. They would have to have a king to lead them in battle.

Israel stamp with picture of King David.

Israeli stamp with picture of King Solomon.

David playing the harp. From an old Jewish manuscript.

The greatest military hero of the time was Saul. He was a young man who had proven himself in battle. He would be their new king, the Israelites decided. In a solemn ceremony, Saul was anointed the king of Israel.

Saul ruled Israel until he was killed in a battle with the Philistines. They were one of the most powerful enemies of the Jews. After Saul's death David became the king. David was a very brave warrior. He was also a talented singer and harp player.

The Reign of King David

Israel grew strong under King David's rule. David conquered much of the enemy territory. The little country became larger and more powerful. King David made Jerusalem the capital of his kingdom. He built palaces for himself and his wives.

27

Although the country flourished, many people were poor. The poor people became angry. They felt the king thought only of his own comfort and did little to make conditions better for them.

Solomon Becomes King

When David died, his son Solomon became king of Israel. Solomon built a beautiful Temple to God in Jerusalem. He wanted the people to come to Jerusalem and take part in the Temple ceremonies.

Solomon also built palaces and fortified cities. He taxed the people very heavily. He forced the Israelites to build the palaces and the forts. The people became very angry at King Solomon.

When Solomon died, several of the tribes would not swear allegiance to his son. They formed their own kingdom. They called it Israel. The country ruled by Solomon's son was called Judah. So there were now two Jewish kingdoms in the land of Israel. Each kingdom had its own territory. And each was ruled by its own king.

Soon these two kingdoms grew weak. They had been strong when they were united. But as two kingdoms they were conquered by neighboring nations. The ten tribes which made up the kingdom of Israel were never heard from again. We call them the ten lost tribes. The tribes of Judah and Levi were exiled to Babylonia. They became the forefathers of the Jewish people.

The Prophets

During this time, the religious life of the Jews was changing. The changes were very important. They were brought about by a group of religious leaders called prophets. The prophets were men of force and action. They were religious leaders and patriots who loved their people, the land of Israel and its traditions. They fought to keep the people loyal to the religion of their fathers. This meant that idol worship was to be wiped out. Justice and honesty was to be the law of the land. The prophets fought for the rights of the widow, the orphan and all unfortunate and poor people.

Perhaps you already know about some of the prophets. Their preachings are found in the Bible. You may have read about some of the prophets in your Bible stories.

Isaiah was one of the best-known prophets. He taught of a time when the whole world would live in peace. He wrote:

In the end of days . . . they shall beat their swords
into plowshares, and their spears into pruning hooks;
nation shall not make war upon nation, neither shall they learn war any more.

Another prophet, Micah, wrote:

What does God want of you—to do justly, to love mercy, and to walk humbly with your God.

Perhaps you will want to learn these writings by heart. Find the teachings of the prophets in the Bible. Ezekiel, Amos, Jonah, and Zechariah are other prophets you may want to look up.

The words of the prophets are beautiful and inspiring. It would have been wonderful if the people took them to heart and did as the prophets preached. But many did not. Even today we do not have the peace and goodness that these religious leaders spoke about. Perhaps someday we will.

UNIT III

WHY JEWS LIVE IN MANY LANDS

Italians live in Italy, Germans in Germany, Canadians in Canada, the Irish in Ireland, the Dutch in Holland, the Mexicans in Mexico. But Jews live in almost every corner of the world. They live in Israel and the United States. They live in England and in Russia. They live in India, South Africa, Brazil, and France. Jews live in many other countries throughout the world.

Have you ever wondered why this is so? Once all Jews lived in the country we now call Israel. Now they are scattered all over the world.

In this unit you will find out why. You will go back again to the beginning of Jewish history. You will find out why the Jews left their homeland. We will follow the Jews of old to different lands. You will see how they fared in some of these countries. You will learn of the contributions that they made in these different countries.

The Jews of old developed two separate traditions, the Ashkenazic and the Sephardic. But in spite of this, and in spite of living in many different lands, they continued to be one people. They were unified in spirit. And they were unified in belief. The Jews preserved their religion wherever they lived. Now you will find out how they were able to do so.

chapter 8

Going Back into Ancient History

In the last unit you read that the ancestors of the Jewish people lived in their own land, the country that is now called Israel. They had their own customs. They had their own religion and their own government. They also had their own kings who ruled over them.

The religion of the Jews of long ago was in many ways different from that of Jews now. The God they served was the same God Jews worship today. But

An Israelite stone altar found at Meggido, Israel. Notice the four horns at the corners of the altar.

how they observed their religion was quite different. They did not worship in a synagogue as Jews do today. They sacrificed animals at a shrine in Jerusalem. This shrine was called the Holy House (Bet Hamikdash) or Temple.

People who lived far away from Jerusalem came to the Temple. At the Temple they would sacrifice and rededicate themselves to God. Remember, in those days travel was very slow. They had to leave their homes many weeks before the holiday. Some came on foot and some rode. The trip had to be made.

Everyone wanted to participate in the ceremonies in the Bet Hamikdash. At the Temple they would sacrifice. They would rededicate themselves to God. The Temple was very important to the Jews.

A reconstruction of Solomon's Temple.

An obelisk is a four-sided stone monument which comes to a point. This obelisk was erected in honor of Shalmaneser III, king of Assyria. One of the panels shows Jehu, king of Israel, surrendering to the Assyrian king. Jehu is on his knees, bowing before the victorious Shalmaneser.

Their religion was centered around it. Three times a year, on the holidays of Passover, Shavuoth, and Succoth, they

In this panel Jehu, the king of Israel, is on his knees bowing before the victorious Shalmaneser.

would make trips to the Temple. These trips were called pilgrimages.

Life in those days was hard for the Jews. Israel was surrounded by unfriendly neighbors even as it is today. Sometimes it was conquered by a powerful enemy. When this happened, many of the strong young men and women were carried off as slaves to the foreign country. Sometimes people fled to friendly countries. They wanted to escape being conquered. In this way, small Jewish communities began to establish themselves in some of the countries near Israel.

The Jews in Babylonia

About 2,600 years ago there was a great and powerful nation in the Middle East. Babylonia was this country. Nebuchadnezzar was its king. Under his rule many nations were conquered. When a country was conquered, the captives were taken back to Babylonia. This was done to make sure that there were not enough strong young people left behind to rebel against the Babylonians.

Nebuchadnezzar captured Jerusalem and captured King Jehoiachin of Judah. This tablet dates from the period of Nebuchadnezzar. It mentions the fall and the ruin of Jerusalem and also tells about the capture of the king.

This seal impression was found on a clay jar handle. It is from the time of King Jehoiachin of Judah. It reads "belonging to Eliakin the servant of Jehoiachin."

In the year 586 B.C.E. Babylonia conquered the tiny Jewish kingdom of Judah. The Babylonians destroyed the Bet Hamikdash (the Temple). They carried off many brave young men and women.

How sad the captives were in Babylonia. Their homes and families were in Judah. They feared they would no longer be able to serve God. God's House had been destroyed. They were dejected. An unknown Jewish poet expressed their feelings.

By the waters of Babylon,
There we sat down and wept,
When we remembered Zion [Israel].

This poem is in the Bible. It is in the Book of Psalms.

The king of Babylonia was very powerful. His name was Nebuchadnezzar. His country conquered many other surrounding nations as well as Israel. Nebuchadnezzar ruled over all of them.

A copy of an Assyrian relief showing plunder being removed from a defeated city.

King Nebuchadnezzar admired the Jews in many ways even though he had conquered them. He selected a group of Jewish young men to serve in his palace. The men he selected were the most handsome, intelligent, and strongest of all his Jewish captives. One of them was named Daniel. Daniel grew up to be one of the king's most important advisors.

This story, and others as well, is told in the Book of Daniel in the Bible.

The Book of Daniel is a very important written record that helps us to understand the Babylonian captivity of the Jews. Perhaps you will want to read this book of the Bible. It is not too long, and in it you will find many interesting stories about Daniel, and also about King Nebuchadnezzar and the kings who came after him.

The Jews who were forced to live in Babylonia did not forget about their God. Nor did they forget their religion. In the next chapter you will see how they retained their faith. In 539 B.C.E., when a new king allowed them to return to their homeland, many Jews wanted to remain in Babylonia. They were prosperous and happy in their new country. However, while many Jews continued to live in Babylonia, a great number did return to their homeland.

It was the policy of the Babylonian kings to destroy the cities that they captured. The leaders were killed or deported and the city walls destroyed. This is a wall of stone blocks, some of the remains of the ancient walls of Jerusalem.

End of Jewish Independence

The Jews who returned to the land of Israel had two main tasks. They wanted to re-establish their religion. They had to make their country strong again. They did not want to be attacked by neighboring countries. The first Jews who returned from Babylonia rebuilt the Bet Hamikdash. Their leader was named Zerubbabel. Soon after the Jews in Israel had two other great leaders, Ezra and Nehemiah.

Ezra was the religious leader. He knew that the Jews had forgotten most of their religious laws and customs. If the Jewish religion was to be observed, the laws and customs had to be learned again. He called all the people to come to Jerusalem. There Ezra read the Torah and explained the customs to them. When Ezra finished, the people fasted. They prayed and they promised to follow the laws of the Torah for the rest of their lives.

The Ishtar Gate in the ancient city of Babylon. The animals on the wall are bulls, lions, and dragons. The designs are made of bricks covered with colored glazes.

The armies of Babylon were defeated by the Persians. The Persians were good to the Jews of Babylon and Israel. They allowed Ezra and many Jews to return. Persian soldiers escorted the Jews. These are Persian soldiers. They are armed with spears and bows and arrows.

Nehemiah was the political leader of the Jews. It was his job to rebuild the country. He had to make sure that the people would be able to govern themselves.

All the people joined together to rebuild the walls of Jerusalem. Priests, merchants, children, and women helped. It took many days to rebuild the walls. When they finished, Jerusalem was safe again.

Remains of an ancient building in Israel.

Egyptians, and then it was ruled by the Syrians. At first the Jews lived peacefully under Syrian rule. They adopted many of the Greek customs that the Syrians followed. Some even gave their children Greek names. And some followed parts of the Greek religion.

After a number of years there was a new Syrian king. His name was Antiochus Epiphanes. He was a tyrant. He wanted all the Jews to behave like Greeks. He put statues of Zeus in the Temple. He ordered all the Jews to worship Zeus. Those who did not obey were put to death.

The rest of the story is well known. Mattathias stood up to the king's soldiers. He asked all who were faithful to God to follow him. His five sons, with Judah Maccabee at their head, led the rebellion against Syria. They won their

A Greek soldier under attack. He wears a metal helmet and breastplate. This painting was found on an ancient stone coffin.

For about 200 years, the Jews lived in peace. They took care of their farms and their flocks. They raised families and taught their children the laws of the Torah. They prayed at the Bet Hamikdash, they studied Torah and kept the laws.

But the peace did not last. Israel was ruled first by the Persians, then by the

An enameled picture of Judah Maccabee. It was painted in the 15th century by a French painter.

Portrait coin of Emperor Vespasian, the conqueror of Jerusalem, 69-79 C.E.

independence from the Syrian tyrant, Antiochus.

The hard-won freedom and peace did not last for very long. The Jews began to quarrel among themselves. Political and religious parties arose. Each party had its own idea of what was good for the country. And each thought it knew what God expected from the people. The Jewish rulers were corrupt and power-hungry. They oppressed the people. They thought only of themselves. Sometimes there were fights within the ruling family over who would hold power. Sometimes one brother killed another so he could gain control of the country.

These conditions made the Jews weak and powerless. At that time the Romans were a powerful people in the world. It was easy for them to gain control of the land of the Jews, which in those days was called Judea. But the Jews were used to being free. Many other nations accepted Roman rule. But the Jews would not. There were many battles with the Romans. But the Jews could not win. The Romans were too strong.

The Roman governors forced the Jews to pay heavy taxes. They tried to make the Jews worship Roman gods. Many Jews would not obey. They organized themselves into bands of rebels called Zealots. The Zealots fought against the Romans. They did not obey the Roman laws. Many Zealots were arrested and killed. But this made the others even angrier. They fought even harder against the Romans.

In 66 C.E. war broke out between Rome and the Jews. It was a brutal war—a war without mercy. One of the generals of the Judean army was named Josephus. He became a traitor and sided with Rome. He tried to convince the Zealots to give up, but they would not. The Zealots continued to fight very hard, just like the Maccabees two hundred years earlier.

The Jews were very brave and they fought very hard. But they were not successful. The Romans were too powerful for them. One fortress after another was captured.

Josephus before Emperor Vespasian, from a twelfth-century manuscript.

To celebrate the capture of Jerusalem the Roman conquerors built an arch in Rome. This monument is called the Arch of Titus.

Soon only Jerusalem and Masada remained in Jewish hands. Vespasian, the emperor of Rome, sent his son, Titus, to conquer Jerusalem. Jerusalem was very strong. It was very well fortified. Three rows of heavy walls surrounded it. Inside the city there were almost a million people. They fought very hard against the Romans. But they also fought among themselves. There were many disagreements about the way to fight the Romans. Titus waited. He knew that soon the Jews would grow weak. The internal fighting, hunger, and disease would make it easy to conquer the city. He was right. In the year 70 C.E. the Romans captured Jerusalem. The Romans then destroyed the Holy Temple.

Now only the fortress of Masada remained. You read about it in an earlier unit. The 960 Zealots who defended Masada would not give up. They killed themselves rather than be conquered and enslaved by the Romans. With the fall of Masada, the Romans were in complete control of the land of Israel. Sixty years later there was another Jewish revolt against Rome, led by Simon Bar-Kochba. This too ended in a Jewish defeat.

For two thousand years thereafter, the Jews did not have a land of their own. Many remained in Israel, but most went to live in other lands throughout the world.

In later units, you will follow the Jews from country to country. You will see how they managed to hold on to their religion. You will see that they observed their religion and kept the laws of the Torah in every country in which they lived.

A copy of the carving on the Arch of Titus, showing the Menorah and other furniture of the Temple being carried in triumph through the streets of Rome.

chapter 9

A Portable Religion

When the Romans conquered Jerusalem, the Temple was destroyed. The Jews no longer had a country of their own. They no longer had a king. They no longer had their religious shrine, the Bet Hamikdash.

If you were to study the history of other nations, you would see that under just such conditions many nations simply ceased to exist. They were never heard from again. This did not happen to the Jews. If it had, you would not be

A relief is a deep carving on a flat surface. This stone relief of the holy Ark was found in the ancient synagogue at Capernaum, Israel. The carving is about 2,500 years old.

A clay oil lamp about 2,000 years old. It has a design of the Temple Menorah.

here today reading about the Jewish religion. You would not be reading about the history of the Jewish people. What made it possible for the Jewish religion and the Jewish people to survive?

Judaism survived under such difficult conditions because it had developed a religious tradition that could be followed anywhere in the world. It was not limited to the Bet Hamikdash in Jerusalem. In other words, the Jews had developed what we might call a "portable religion." One that could be "carried" with them wherever they lived.

Now you will see exactly how this happened. The Jews developed two important institutions that made this possible: the synagogue and the Oral Law. Each of these will be discussed

The ancient synagogue of Capernaum on the shores of the Sea of Galilee, Israel.

The Babylonian study groups made it possible for the Jewish captives to keep their religion alive until they could return to their homeland. When the Jews returned to Israel in 539 B.C.E. Ezra continued the small group gatherings. He set up meeting houses. Here people could gather to worship and study between visits to the Bet Hamikdash to sacrifice. The meeting houses were helpful to the people who lived far away from the Temple. It was hard for them to make frequent visits to the Bet Hamikdash. But now they could still practice their religion. They could remain faithful Jews.

Many towns built their own houses of prayer. In these houses of prayer the

The mosaic floor of the synagogue at Bet Alpha, Israel. The round panel shows the symbols of the zodiac. The names are in Hebrew. This mosaic is about 2,500 years old. A mosaic is a picture made by placing small pieces of colored glass or stone in cement.

separately. You will see how they made it possible for Judaism to continue after the Temple was destroyed.

The Synagogue

In ancient days Jewish religious life was centered around the Bet Hamikdash. The people worshipped by offering animal sacrifices to God. These sacrifices were offered for the people by the priests.

When the Jews were exiled to Babylonia in 586 B.C.E., a new form of religious life began to develop. The people wanted to study their traditions. They wanted to worship God. They began to gather in small groups. They studied and worshipped. These small study groups were the earliest synagogues. From them developed the synagogues and temples of our own day.

priests taught the Torah and instructed the people how to observe the festivals. Here the people met to celebrate the Sabbath and holidays, to conduct their meetings and discuss their community problems. Here judges held court, and here marriages were celebrated. These houses of worship and learning, these centers of community life, became what we now call synagogues.

The second Bet Hamikdash was destroyed by Rome in 70 C.E. Thousands of Jews were taken captive and forced to live in many different countries. The idea of the meeting house, or synagogue, went with them. It made it possible for them to remain good and loyal Jews no matter where they lived. Up to our own time, the synagogue (or temple) has made it possible for Jews to live as Jews. It has made it possible for Jews to remember their traditions. Whether large or small, ornate or simple, the synagogue remains the most important institution in Jewish life.

At first, as we saw in earlier units, the Jews had a country of their own—the land of Israel. Later on they had to live in many different countries. Their way of life changed. But two things helped them to survive as Jews. The synagogue gave them a place to meet and worship even after the Temple was destroyed. The Oral Law made it possible to figure out new ways to follow the Torah even in different countries and different times.

The Oral Law

The study groups and synagogues provided a place to worship God. But the Jews needed one more thing to hold them together, one more thing to keep them loyal to their religion. They needed religious laws—laws that could be followed in any land in which they lived, laws that could be followed at any time in history. The Oral Law was just that.

To understand the Oral Law, it will help if you understand something about the laws of our country, the United States of America. The government of the United States operates according to law. This is one of the reasons that America is a strong, stable country. The basis, or foundation, of America's laws is provided by the Constitution. This document sets forth all the important things Americans believe in. It outlines the way we want our country to be run. It also tells us how to change our laws when necessary.

The Constitution itself does not change—except in unusual cases when it is amended—but our understandings of the Constitution do change. New and different laws are sometimes needed. Even so, the Constitution remains the basis for the new laws. It provides us with a guideline for determining whether the new laws agree with the principles on which America was founded. The Constitution allows us to change our laws when necessary, but in a way that does not threaten our basic beliefs and values.

Long before there was a United States or an American Constitution, the Jews developed a similar way of changing their laws and keeping them up to date. They did this by means of the Oral Law.

The written foundation of Jewish law is the Torah. The role of the Torah in Jewish society is something like that of the Constitution in American society. The Torah contains the main principles and ideas of Judaism. All Jewish laws are based on the Torah.

The Oral Law existed side by side with the written Torah. The Oral Law consisted of discussions of the Torah by many generations of Jewish scholars. These rabbis tried to understand what the laws in the Torah meant. They tried to find ways of carrying out the laws in the Torah in different times and circumstances. When they came up with new ways of carrying out the laws in the Torah, their new approaches were solidly based on the laws and principles in the Torah, just as America's laws are solidly based on the laws and principles in the Constitution.

For many centuries the Oral Law was not written down (hence its name—*oral* means "spoken"). It was memorized by the rabbis and passed on orally from generation to generation. In time the Oral Law became so large that it was necessary to write it down. This happened around 200 C.E. The written version of the Oral Law is called the Mishnah.

In the centuries that followed, new generations of rabbis studied the laws in the Mishnah. Their discussions were gathered together with the Mishnah in an even larger collection of laws called the Talmud. Actually there are two Talmuds—one containing the discussions of the rabbis in Babylonia, the other containing the discussions of the rabbis in the land of Israel—but both include the same Mishnah.

The Talmud is a vast collection of laws and discussions. The subjects it covers include farming, prayer, medicine, astronomy and science, holidays, marriage and divorce, Shabbat, business matters, crime and punishment, government, and just about anything else you can think of. It is estimated that the Babylonian Talmud has about two million words. In its printed edition, it covers 5,894 large-sized pages.

A page from the Mishnah. The Mishnah is at the top of the page. To the right and left are commentaries (explanations) of the text.

The Talmud is made up of two different kinds of writings. They are called Halacha and Aggada. Halacha is law. Most of the Talmud—about two-thirds—is made up of laws. This is considered the more important part of the Talmud.

Aggada means "tales." The Aggada is made up of legends, debates, wise sayings, medical advice, and even humor. These were used by the scholars of the Talmud to make special points. One well-known story in the Aggada is a fable about a fox and some fish. You will enjoy reading it. See if you can figure out the point it makes.

It was a bad time for the Jews. They were not permitted to study or teach the Torah. Akiba, a famous rabbi, continued to teach the Torah. His students did not understand. They asked Akiba,

"Aren't you afraid you'll be killed?" Akiba answered by telling this story.

Once there was a sly and hungry fox. As he walked along the seashore he saw some fish swimming in the water. They were scurrying to and fro and seemed confused and frightened.

"What is the matter?" asked the fox. "What are you afraid of?"

We are afraid of the fishermen's nets," answered the fish.

"Come out of the water and I will take care of you," said the sly fox.

"Oh no," said the fish. "If we are not safe in the water, which is our natural place, how can we be safe out of water, where there are even more dangers?"

Do you understand the point the scholars were trying to make when they told this story?

Here are some wise sayings from the

A page from the Soncino Talmud. The whole Talmud has been translated into English.

liability], with the remark, 'What could he have done? [93b] He guarded [them] as people guard.'¹ Abaye protested, 'If so, had he entered the town when people generally enter it [leaving his charges alone], would he still be exempt?' – 'Yes', he replied. 'Then had he slept a little when other people sleep, would he also be exempt?' – 'Even so,' was his answer. Thereupon he raised an objection: The following are the accidents for which a paid bailee is not responsible: E.g., *And the Sabeans fell upon them* [sc. the oxen and asses], *and took them away; yea, they have slain the servants with the edge of the sword.*⁴ – He replied, 'There the reference is to city watchmen.'⁵

He further raised an objection: To what extent is a paid bailee bound to guard? Even as far as, *Thus I was; in the day the drought consumed me, and the frost by night?*⁶ – There too, he answered, the reference is to the city watchman. Was then our father Jacob a city watchman? he asked. – [No.] He merely said to Laban, 'I guarded for you with super-vigilance, as though I were a city watchman.'

He raised another objection: If a shepherd, who was guarding his flock, left it and entered the town, and a wolf came and destroyed [a sheep]; or a lion, and tore it to pieces, we do not say, 'Had he been there, he could have saved them;' but estimate his strength: if he could have saved them, he is responsible; if not, he is exempt.⁷ Surely it means that he entered [the town] when other people generally do? – No. He entered when people do not generally enter. If so, why is he not responsible? Where there is negligence in the beginning, though subsequently an accident supervenes, he is liable!¹ – It means that he heard the voice of a lion, and so entered. If so, why judge his strength? What could he then have done? – He should have met it with [the assistance of other] shepherds and staves. If so, why particularly a paid bailee? The same applies even to an unpaid one. For you yourself, Master, did say: If an unpaid bailee could have met [the destroyer, e.g., a lion] with other shepherds and staves, but did not, he is responsible! – An unpaid bailee [must obtain their help only when he can procure them] gratuitously; whereas a paid bailee must even [engage them] for payment. And to what extent?² – Up to their value.³ But where do we find that a paid trustee is responsible for accidents?⁴ – Subse-

but none pay heed to them,' he replied.

Aibu entrusted flax to Ronia. Then Shabu¹⁰ came and stole it b from him;¹ but subsequently the thief's identity became known. Then he [the trustee] came before R. Nahman, who ruled him liable.² Shall we say that he disagrees with R. Huna b. Abin. For R. Huna b. Abin sent word:³ If it [the bailment] was stolen through an accident, and then the thief's identity became known, if he was a gratuitous bailee, he can either swear [that he had not been negligent] or settle with him;⁴ if a paid trustee, he must settle with him, and cannot swear! – Said Raba: There,⁵ officers were about, and had he [Ronia] cried out, they would have come and protected him.⁶

MISHNAH. [If] one wolf [attacks], it is not an unavoidable accident;⁷ if two [attack], it is an unavoidable accident. R. Judah said: When there is a general visitation of wolves, even [the attack of] one is an unavoidable accident.⁸ [the attack of] two dogs is not an unavoidable accident. Jaddua the Babylonian said on R. Meir's authority: if they attack from the same side, it is not an unavoidable accident; from two different directions, it is. A robber's [attack] is an unavoidable accident. [damage done by] a lion, bear, leopard, panther and snake ranks as an unavoidable accident. when is this? if they came [and attacked] of their own accord; but if he [the shepherd] led them to a place infested by wild beasts and robbers, it is no unavoidable accident. if it died a natural death, it is an unavoidable accident; [but] if he maltreated it¹ and it died, it is no unavoidable accident. if it ascended to the top of steep rocks and then fell down, it is an unavoidable accident; but if he took it up to the top of steep rocks and it fell and died, it is no unavoidable accident.

Aggada. You have heard some of them before, but did you know they were from the Talmud? See how many you can recognize.

- The treament of a doctor who does not charge a fee is not worth anything.
- When in Rome do as the Romans do.
- Who is wise? He who learns from everyone.
- Who is rich? He who is satisfied with what he has.
- Opportunity knocks at least once for everyone.
- The walls have ears.
- Who is a fool? He who loses what is given to him.

As you can see, there is a great deal of wisdom in the Talmud in addition to the laws.

You first read about the Talmud in chapter 2 of Unit I. There it was described as an important written record that helps us to understand the history of the Jews. But it is also important to understand the Talmud as an important religious tradition. It has had a great deal of influence, not only on the Jews at the time when it was first developed, but also on Jewish life ever since.

Through the ages Jewish scholars have studied the Talmud. They have written long explanations of different statements and ideas in the Talmud. These explanations are called commentaries. Even in our own time a person who wants to become a rabbi studies these laws written long ago. Many Jews believe that all Jews must follow all the laws in the Talmud if they are to be considered good Jews. But others do not. They believe that the laws of the Talmud were important at the time they were written, but now we live in a different time, and the laws of the Talmud must continue to change with the times.

Students studying the Talmud

UNIT IV

ASHKENAZIC AND SEPHARDIC JEWS

You have probably eaten such foods as gefilte fish, blintzes, chicken–matzah ball soup, stuffed cabbage, and bagels and lox. They are considered to be typically Jewish foods. But have you ever eaten moussaka, goats' cheese, medyas, and bahklava? These, too, are considered to be typically Jewish foods by some Jews. The Jews whose tradition includes such foods as gefilte fish are the Ashkenazim. The Jews whose tradition includes foods like moussaka are the Sephardim.

Jews from Europe speak Yiddish. It is a combination of Hebrew and German. It was developed by the Jews of Poland. To the German they had spoken in Germany, mixed with some Hebrew words, they added Polish words and expressions. This developed into what we know today as Yiddish. But have you ever heard Ladino? That, too, is a Jewish language. It is a combination of Spanish and Hebrew. It was developed by the Sephardic Jews so that they could communicate with each other wherever they lived.

Most American Jews come from Ashkenazic backgrounds. They are familiar with the foods, customs, and language of Ashkenazic Jews. They are not familiar with the foods, customs, and language of Sephardic Jews. Even so, both of these traditions are very important in Jewish history. Both the Sephardim and the Ashkenazim have had a share in making up the fabric of modern Jewish life.

In the next unit you will see how these two traditions developed. Chapters 10, 11, and 12 trace the story of the Sephardic Jews. Chapters 13, 14, 15, 16, and 17 tell about the Ashkenazic Jews and what happened to them.

chapter 10

The Story of the Sephardic Jews

The word *Sephardic* means "Spanish." But the Sephardic Jews are not just Spanish Jews. The word is used to include all Jews whose ancestors lived in Spain a long time ago, as well as those Jews in other countries who follow the traditions started by the Spanish Jews.

In Spain and then in other places, the Sephardic Jews usually lived under the

A scene in a Spanish synagogue, from a very old Haggadah. In Sephardic synagogues, the reader's desk is always in the center of the synagogue. Note the people surrounding the reader's desk.

influence of the Arabic-Moslem culture, just as the Ashkenazic Jews lived under the influence of Christian European culture. The Moslem Arabs of many years ago were well educated. They were highly advanced in science, mathematics, literature, and philosophy. The Jews who lived among them added to this vast storehouse of knowledge. They also learned much from their Arab neighbors. For many years the Arabs and the Jews lived together in peace. They learned from each other. They helped each other. And they benefitted greatly from their association.

The Sephardic tradition started in Spain and Portugal. Then it spread to other countries. You will read what happened to the Jews in Spain in the next chapter.

First let us go back to Israel. Let's see what happened to the Jews after the conquest by Rome. For a few hundred years after the fall of Jerusalem, some Jews continued to live in and around Israel. Others moved to Jewish communities in such places as Babylonia, Syria, Egypt, and Greece. Cultural and educational centers were established in these countries. The Jews mingled freely with the surrounding peoples. But they retained their religious beliefs. And they kept their Jewish way of life. The Talmud was developed in Babylonia and in Israel. Long before this the Greek Jews had translated the Bible into Greek.

But then two events occurred which changed the course of world history and had a great effect on Jewish life. Two new religions were born. They were both related to Judaism. They were Christianity and Islam (or Mohammedanism). These two religions spread in different parts of the world. Christianity spread to Italy, France, Germany, Britain, and the other countries of Europe. Islam spread to North Africa, the Arab countries of the Middle East, and Spain. The Ashkenazim lived in the countries controlled by Christians. The Sephardim lived in countries controlled by Moslems (Moslems are followers of the religion of Islam).

The holy city of Mecca and its mosque. Near the center of the mosque is a small shrine called the Kaaba. Moslems believe that the Kaaba was built by Abraham and Ishmael. Embedded in one wall of the Kaaba is a black stone. Moslems believe the stone was given to Adam by an angel. Each year thousands of Moslem pilgrims come from far away to kiss the sacred black stone.

The Koran is regarded by Moslems as God's word. The Koran consists of 114 chapters called surahs. This is a page from a very old Koran written in an early form of Arabic script.

Sephardic Jews have lived in North Africa. They have lived in Iraq, Turkey, Palestine, Greece, Italy, and Holland. At the present time there are Sephardic communities in the United States and in Israel. They are also in South America, Greece, Turkey, and in some of the Arab countries. Wherever they live they continue to follow their own customs. Their synagogues and prayers are different from those of the Ashkenazim. They follow the custom of naming their children after living rela-

Islam, like Christianity, is based on the Hebrew Bible. This old Moslem manuscript pictures Adam and Eve in the Garden of Eden.

tives, instead of after those who have died as do the Ashkenazic Jews. The last names of the Sephardim are often Arabic, Spanish, Greek, or Italian. They do not even sound Jewish to Jews of East European origin. Some Sephardim speak Ladino. Many others speak Arabic, the language of the countries in which their ancestors lived for many generations. They continue to eat the foods that they learned to prepare in the exotic countries of the East.

In the next chapter you will read about the great Sephardic community that developed in Moslem Spain. The Jews who lived there were prosperous. They were well educated. They were influential in government affairs. You will read about what happened to them. You will also read about the contributions they made to their country and to Jewish life.

A Jewish man from Constantinople, Turkey, 1700.

A young Jewish woman from Morocco, 1700.

Blue and purple costumes worn by Turkish Jews about 200 years ago.

chapter 11

The Jews of Spain

In Newport, Rhode Island, there is a very old synagogue. It is the oldest synagogue in the United States. This synagogue is called the Touro Synagogue. It was built by American Jews whose ancestors were Spanish Jews. It was built in the early days of our country. This synagogue has a very unusual feature. In the floor of the pulpit there is a trapdoor. It leads to a secret passageway.

How strange to see a trapdoor in a synagogue. But the door is there for a good reason. It was put there by the founders. They wanted to be reminded that their ancestors were not always free to worship as they wished. Many Jews were driven out of Spain in 1492. Others stayed, but they were forced to convert to Christianity. Many of them only pretended to convert, but practiced the Jewish religion in secret. They were called Marranos, or secret Jews. Their places of worship often had trapdoors leading to secret passageways. This way they could escape if the police came to investigate.

This was a very sad time in the history of the Jews of Spain. You will read more about it later in this chapter. The story of the Spanish Jews begins at a time when they lived at peace with their neighbors, at a time when Jewish life flourished in Spain.

In Early Days

The Jews first came to Spain many years ago. They came as long as two thousand years ago. They were well treated. And they prospered. Many of them became farmers. Others engaged in trade. Some became public officials.

For many years the Jews lived in Spain. There were bad times as well as good. But on the whole Jewish life in Spain was peaceful and comfortable. Many Jews were wealthy. Some even had high government positions. One of these was Hasdai Ibn Shaprut. He was a doctor. He became the chief advisor to the caliph, or ruler.

Hasdai was the son of a wealthy and scholarly Jew. When he was young, he studied Hebrew, Arabic, and Latin. He learned these languages thoroughly. He also studied medicine. He became an outstanding doctor. His ability as a doctor was so great that he was appointed physician to the caliph.

Hasdai was not only an excellent doctor. He was a wise scholar. He was also a man of great charm, character, and integrity. These traits soon endeared him to the caliph. He became the ruler's chief advisor. As such his position was very powerful. He was the minister of foreign affairs. He arranged treaties with foreign powers. He received the envoys sent by other governments to Spain.

In all that Hasdai did, he remained loyal to the Jewish people and to Judaism. He helped Jews in other countries as well as his own. He was also interested in Jewish scholarship. He sent rich presents to help support the great academies of Jewish learning.

Hasdai was a scientist, a poet, a philanthropist, and a scholar. He was loved and respected by all. He brought great pride to his people.

The Golden Age of Spain

Life continued to be prosperous and peaceful for the Jews of Spain. They became influential in every area of life. Some were active in the army. Others were bankers or scientists. Many were physicians. And many were university professors. Still others were merchants or diplomats. This was a very productive period of Jewish history. Historians call it the Golden Age of Spain.

During this time there was a rebirth of Jewish literature. Books were written by Jews on religious beliefs, on grammar, on astronomy, on mathematics, on medicine, and on many other subjects. Poetry was the most important literary work. Many beautiful poems were written by Jewish poets.

Yehuda Halevi was one of the most famous Jewish poets. When he was young he wrote about love and pleasure. As he grew older his thoughts turned to Israel, which had once been the homeland of the Jews. He longed to travel to that country and live there. He hoped that someday it would again be a Jewish nation.

Yehuda Halevi's love of Israel became the most important thing in his life. He could think of nothing else. His beautiful poems expressed his longing to return to the land of his forefathers. Many of them are among the most touching poems ever written in the Hebrew language.

Abraham Zacuto (1450–1515), famous Jewish astronomer and historian, who fled Portugal to escape the Inquisition and settled in Amsterdam.

In one of them he wrote:

Beautiful land,
Delight of the world,
City of Kings,
My heart longs for you,
From the far-off West.
I am very sad,
When I remember how you were.
Now your glory is gone,
Your homes destroyed.
If I could fly to you
On the wings of eagles,
I would soak your soil,
With my tears.

When Yehuda Halevi was an old man he did finally go to Jerusalem. But the city was not the one of his dreams. It was a dirty, uncultivated city under Arab rule. How disappointed he was. He stood beside the Western Wall of the ancient Bet Hamikdash and wept. As he wept an Arab on a horse stumbled over him. Yehuda Halevi was crushed to death. What a sad ending to his life and his dreams.

Solomon Ibn Gabirol was another great poet. He wrote poetry in Hebrew on many subjects. But he is best known for his beautiful religious poetry. "Early Will I Seek Thee" is one of his most inspirational poems. Many congregations sing it at Friday night services.

Solomon was also an important philosopher. He wrote interesting books and poems in which he described his philosophy about God and the nature of the universe.

This is an inside view of the Santa Maria la Blanca church in Toledo, Spain. This church was at one time a synagogue.

A Spanish-Jewish doctor prescribes medicines to his patients. Notice the medicine chest in the background.

Although Solomon Ibn Gabirol wrote beautiful poetry and important books on philosophy, he was very poor all his life. Other poets and authors helped him with gifts of money. But it still was not enough for his needs. Solomon was never able to marry because he was too poor to support a wife. He died when he was a very young man. His life was sad and short, but his writings were beautiful and important.

There were hard times in Spain as well as good. In the year 1148 the city of Cordova was conquered by Moslem fanatics who tried to convert everyone to their version of Islam. Many Jews left Spain rather than give up their religion.

Among those who left was the family of Moses Maimonides. He was to become one of the most famous Jewish doctors and scholars of all time. When he left Cordova with his family, Moses was only thirteen years old. He and his family wandered from country to country looking for a new home.

After a number of years they finally settled in Cairo, Egypt, where Moses became a physician. So well did he do in this profession that he soon became the doctor of Sultan Saladin and the royal family. Moses Maimonides wrote books on asthma, poisons, hygiene, and many other medical subjects.

Israeli stamp with picture of Rabbi Moses ben Maimon (Maimonides).

The Mishneh Torah **is a book of Jewish law written by Moses Maimonides. This is a page from an illustrated German edition of the** Mishneh Torah, **1296.**

A mahzor, or prayer book for Yom Kippur, of a type used by the Sephardic Jews in Portugal and Spain. It is believed that the book was made in this long narrow shape so that it could be quickly hidden in a sleeve in case of a raid by agents of the Inquisition while secret High Holiday services were being held.

Maimonides was known all over the world. The Jews lovingly called him Rambam. This name came from the first letters of his Hebrew name, *R*abbi *M*oshe *b*en *M*aimon.

Although Maimonides was a busy and successful doctor, he also found time to write books on the Jewish religion, the Bible, and science. He was one of the most outstanding rabbis of all time, and his works are still read and studied by Jewish students.

One of the most important works written by Maimonides was the *Mishneh Torah*, or "second Torah." It listed all the

Holograph (a page written in the original handwriting of the author), of Maimonides. This is a page of the Guide to the Perplexed, written in Arabic in Hebrew letters by the Rambam himself.

Jew to be able to understand the laws. So he wrote the *Mishneh Torah* in Hebrew, a language that most Jews understood, and not in Arabic, which he used in writing his other books, because many Jews did not understand Arabic. He also organized the laws in such a way as to make them easier to understand. He divided the laws

Portrait of Maimonides.

Calle de Maimonides, Cordova, Spain.

משע דרכ מיימון

The autograph of Maimonides.

laws of the Talmud that had to do with daily life and religious observance. It also had much good advice about eating and exercise because Moses Maimonides believed that it was a religious duty to stay healthy.

Sometimes books of law are hard to read and follow. But Maimonides wanted every into fourteen topics. Each topic is in a separate volume. That way it is easy to find exactly the law one is looking for.

Moses Maimonides, also known as Rambam, is considered by many Jews to be one of the greatest scholars who ever lived. He is often called the second Moses. It is said of him that "from Moses to Moses there was never one like Moses."

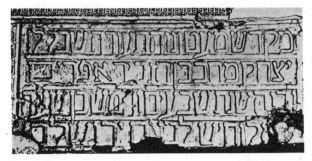

Stone inscription from a fourteenth-century synagogue in Cordova, Spain. The inscription identifies the builder of the synagogue as Isaac Maheb and the year 1315.

The gravestone of a grandson of Moses Maimonides, found in Cairo, Egypt. Because of the greatness of the Rambam, the inscription reads: "This is the grave of David, grandson of Rabbenu the Gaon Moses ben Maimon, Light of the Exile."

Another famous poet of that time was Moses Ibn Ezra. He was born in Granada and belonged to one of the most prominent families of Spain. He wrote beautiful poetry, but much of it was sad. Some people think that he was sad because the woman he loved would not marry him.

Moses Ibn Ezra wrote poetry about love, nature, friendship, old age, and death. But he also wrote beautiful religious poetry. Many of his religious poems are called Selichot. They ask for God's forgiveness and mercy. Some of them can be found in the Rosh Hashana and Yom Kippur services.

Page from the first edition of Abraham Ibn Ezra's commentary to the Pentateuch, Naples, 1488 C.E.

These are just five of the important figures who helped to give this period the name of the Golden Age of Spain. In addition to poets there were also great

A map from a Catalonian atlas by the Spanish-Jewish cartographer Abraham Cresques, 1375.

Bible scholars, scientists, doctors, and statesmen. It was one of the happiest and most creative times in all of Jewish history.

The Spanish Inquisition

The good times in Spain did not last. The Moslems who ruled Spain were conquered by the Christians. The Christians became the ruling group. They believed that it was important to make the whole world Christian. They thought that they were showing their loyalty to their religious beliefs by forcing everyone who was not a Christian to convert.

This was a sad time for the Jews. Many were forced to convert. But many who converted only pretended to be Christians. They converted because they did not want to be killed or tortured. In public they practiced the Christian religion. But in the privacy of their homes

The Spanish priests seated on the platform have sentenced two people to death. They are to be burned alive in a public ceremony called an auto-da-fé.

they were Jews. They even held secret worship services. The secret services were held in places that had escape doors.

Tomas de Torquemada, fanatical leader of the Inquisition, which persecuted untold numbers of Jews and Christians in the name of the Catholic Church.

These Jews who followed their religion in secret were called Marranos. In Spanish the word *marrano* means "pig." But we call them secret Jews.

These Jews tried to keep their religion alive in secret.

Sometimes the secret Jews were found out. They were arrested and brought before a religious court called the Inquisition. Those who were found guilty of practicing Judaism were imprisoned or killed.

Conditions became worse and worse in Spain. In 1492 a decree was issued that all Jews must leave the country. The Jews packed a few possessions and

Many Jews held important positions in the courts of the Spanish kings. In this painting a court Jew is shown forced to kneel and accept Christianity. Notice the crossed hands over his heart.

set sail for other lands. Some reached their destinations. They found friendly countries. And they settled there. Others never arrived in more friendly countries. They died on the seas. This ended a glorious chapter in Spanish Jewish history.

Jewish Life in Modern Times

For hundreds of years there was no Jewish life in Spain. Few Jews ever returned there. There were no religious schools. There were no synagogues and only a few rabbis.

But conditions are changing. There are now about nine thousand Jews in Spain. And the community is growing. About three thousand Jews live in Madrid, the capital of Spain. Until recently these Jews held religious services in rented apartments. In 1968 they built a synagogue, the first one built in Spain in six hundred years. Spanish officials attended the dedication. Rabbis came from all over the world. It was an occasion of great rejoicing for the Jews of Spain and for Jews all over the world.

The Jews of Madrid are very proud of their new synagogue. It has a beautiful sanctuary and classrooms. There is a library and a recreation hall. There are rooms for community meetings. Jews everywhere are hopeful that there will be a rebirth of Judaism in this land that once produced such great Jews and so much Jewish learning.

chapter 12
Sephardic Jews in Other Countries

In this chapter you will follow the Jews of Spain after they were driven from that country. You will see what happened to them.

After 1492 the Jews of Spain followed three main paths. Many remained in Spain and continued to practice their religion in secret as Marranos. Others left Spain and were never heard from again. They died either of starvation or from other causes. They never found a new place to live. But the largest group of all survived. They managed to find new homes.

Some of them went to Portugal. The king welcomed them at first. But when

The Marranos established a colony in the Brazilian city of Recife. Soon the Inquisition came to Brazil and many Jews fled. In 1654 twenty-three Jews arrived in New Amsterdam from Recife. This is an artist's impression of Recife, the wall surrounding the colony and the church.

he saw that they would not convert to Christianity, he drove them from his land.

Portrait medal of Dona Gracia Nasi, 1556. Dona Gracia was the widow of a wealthy Portuguese Marrano banker. She fled the Inquisition and settled in Turkey. Dona Gracia used her money and power to help the Jews of Israel. She also supported Marranos who wished to return to Judaism.

Other Jews settled in Palestine. This was the land we now call Israel. The country was ruled by Turkey. Poverty existed everywhere. But the Jews were allowed to live in some measure of peace. Still other Jews settled in other Arab countries, such as Syria and Iraq. They were not welcomed with open arms, but no physical harm was done to them. They lived peacefully.

Other Sephardic Jews settled in Turkey. An important and creative Jewish community developed there.

Christopher Columbus was convinced that he could reach the Orient by sailing westward. He failed to identify America as a new continent.

A large group settled in Holland and in the New World. In 1492 Columbus discovered the New World. That same year the Jews were driven from Spain. The New World served as a refuge for many Jews. It still continues to do so today. The very king and queen who drove the Jews out of Spain, Ferdinand and Isabella, also financed Columbus in his voyage.

The great Jewish community that existed in Spain did not really die. The Jews who left Spain and settled in other countries continued to make important contributions to the countries that welcomed them. New Sephardic communities grew and prospered. Wherever the Sephardic Jews settled they built synagogues. They continued to practice their religion in other countries. They also continued to follow many of the customs they had brought from Spain.

Most of the Jews who left Spain were well educated. They loved poetry and music. Many knew science and mathematics. They brought their knowledge with them to their new countries. The new countries were richer because they were there.

The Jews in Holland

Holland welcomed the Jews who left Spain. Many of them were wealthy and had held important positions in Spain. They brought their wealth, their experience, and their skills with them. The Jews prospered in Holland. And Holland prospered because of the Jews. The Jews became important to the country in trade and commerce. They invested a great deal of money in Dutch colonies in the New World.

The Jews of Holland were wealthy and important. But they did not forget their religion. In 1593 the Jews of

King Ferdinand, Queen Isabella, and Torquemada kneel in prayer. Torquemada was called the Grand Inquisitor. He was in charge of converting the Jews to Christianity.

Amsterdam were given permission to establish a synagogue. Amsterdam is an important city in Holland. How happy the people were. One hundred years after they were driven from Spain, where they had to worship in secret, they now had a beautiful synagogue. Here they could worship God openly and joyously.

The Jews of Holland did not forget their less fortunate brothers in other countries. They used their wealth and influence to help Jews in other lands. England had refused to allow Jews to live within its borders. It was a Dutch rabbi, Manasseh Ben Israel, who convinced England to open its doors to Jews. Rabbi Manasseh was a prominent citizen of Holland. He started the first Hebrew press there. In 1649 England had a new government. Manasseh Ben Israel wrote to the head of the government, Oliver Cromwell. He persuaded Cromwell that the Jews would help to build trade in England just as they had in Holland. As a result Cromwell allowed the Jews to enter England.

The old synagogue in Amsterdam, Holland. Notice that the reader's desk is in the center of the synagogue. This is the style of Sephardic synagogues.

The Jews of Holland also helped the Jews in the New World. When the first Jews came to New Amsterdam, the governor, Peter Stuyvesant, wanted them to leave. But the colony belonged to the Dutch West India Company. Many of the owners of the company were Jewish. They forced Governor Stuyvesant to accept the Jews as citizens of New Amsterdam.

Sephardic Jews in the New World

Some people believe that Christopher Columbus was a Marrano Jew. No one has been able to prove this, but we do know that there were Marranos who were very important in his voyage.

Luis de Santangel was the royal treasurer of Spain. He persuaded King Ferdinand and Queen Isabella to finance

Drawing of Manasseh Ben Israel.

Governor Peter Stuyvesant leading his soldiers on parade. Peter Stuyvesant had a wooden leg.

Isaac Aboab, rabbi in Amsterdam and the first rabbi to come to the western hemisphere. In 1642 he was called to the Dutch Jewish community of Recife, but he returned to Amsterdam when the Portuguese conquered the colony and brought in the Inquisition.

Columbus' trip. Luis de Santangel was a Marrano Jew.

Luis de Torres was an important member of Columbus' crew. He was also a Marrano. The Jews of Spain were important in the discovery of America.

The Sephardic Jews were also important in the development of America. They came to live in the New World in the earliest days of settlement. In 1506 a group of Marranos were permitted by Portugal to go to Brazil, in South America. They established a colony there. These Marranos were the first to cultivate sugar in the New World. To this day, an island in Brazil bears the name of the founder of its first town, Fernando Noronha. He was a Marrano Jew.

But Brazil did not continue to be a haven for Jews. Soon the Inquisition followed the Jews there. Again they had to flee. Some went to other South American countries and to parts of Central America. Others went to New Amsterdam, a Dutch colony in North America. They believed that they would find peace and acceptance.

The first Jews who came to this country were Sephardim. In 1654 twenty-three of them landed in New Amsterdam, which today is New York City. The governor was Peter Stuyvesant. He was not very happy to see them. He did not like Jews under any circumstances. He especially did not like these Jews, who had fled from persecution in Brazil. They were so poor they could not pay for their passage on the ship that had brought them. He thought that they would not be much of an asset to his small, new community.

How wrong he was. There was discrimination against them. But the Jews prospered in New Amsterdam. Soon they became valuable members of the community. They engaged in business. They built a synagogue. Soon they were an integral part of the life of New Amsterdam.

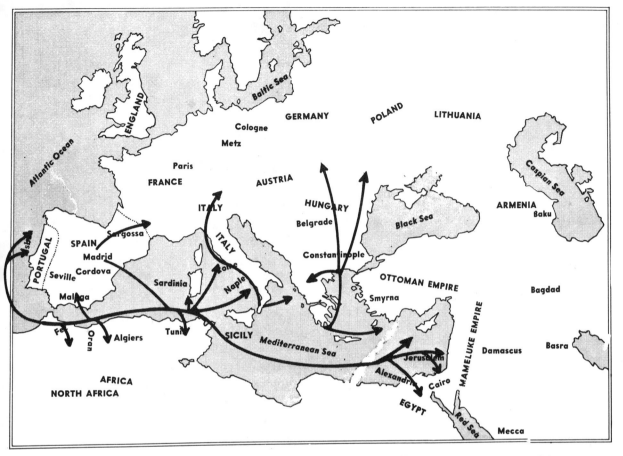

This map shows some of the places, far and near, to which Jews went after the expulsion from Spain. Many went to nearby Portugal, where the Inquisition soon followed them. Others went to North Africa and Egypt, or to Italian cities or further north into Europe. A small group succeeded in returning to Palestine, while large settlements grew up in the east, in cities of the Ottoman Empire.

The Mill Street Synagogue of the Shearith Israel **Congregation of New York, erected in 1730.**

A few years later there was a second Jewish community. It was in Newport, Rhode Island. At that time Rhode Island was the only colony that allowed people to worship as they pleased. Soon the Jews became an important part of the community. Over two hundred years ago they built a synagogue in Newport. That synagogue is now a museum and is used for religious services on special occasions. It is called the Touro Synagogue.

Within a few years there were Jewish settlements in five of the thirteen colonies. When the Revolutionary War started, there were about twenty-five hundred Jews in the American colonies. Many were merchants or traders. They lived mostly in seaport towns. Nearly all the Jews who came to the United States at this time were Sephardic Jews. Ashkenazic Jews did not begin to come to the United States in large numbers until about the 1840s. You will read about them in the next unit.

Aaron Lopez, distinguished citizen of Newport, Rhode Island. He came from a Marrano family in Portugal in 1752.

At the present time, Sephardic Jews live in many countries in Central and South America. And they live in the United States. Wherever they live, they remain good Jews and good citizens.

The Touro Synagogue, Newport, Rhode Island.

chapter 13
The Story of the Ashkenazic Jews

Think about family trees for a moment. The ancestors of most of today's American Jews were of Ashkenazic origin. They came from Germany, Russia, Poland, or some other country in northern or central Europe. Nearly all of the Jews who now live in the United States are descended from Ashkenazic Jews.

The word *Ashkenazic* means "German." The term is used to include all the Jews of Europe who lived in countries where Christianity dominated. *Sephardic* is used to include all Jews who lived in countries where Islam dominated. You will read about the Jews of Germany, Poland, and Russia. You will follow the Ashkenazic Jews. They crossed the Atlantic Ocean and settled in the United States. You will see the strong Jewish community established by American Jews. You will also read about the Jewish communities of present-day Europe. You will see that Jews live peacefully and happily in some countries in Europe. You will also see that there are still countries where Jews are not free. They cannot live according to the teachings of their religion.

Oppression and Persecution

The lives of the Ashkenazic Jews were often sad. They were often dominated by hatred, discrimination, and oppression. Occasionally there were periods of peace. Sometimes there was comparative security. In some countries Jews lived peacefully under the protection of the government or church officials. But these times were brief and far between. Much of the time the Ashkenazic Jews of Europe were despised and persecuted.

Christianity was the dominant religion where the Ashkenazic Jews lived. The Christian religion teaches love and brotherhood. But many people who practiced Christianity did not follow the ideas of peace, love, and brotherhood. They wanted to convert all "non-believers" to Christianity. They hated the Jews. They believed that the Jews had killed Jesus. The Jews had their own religion. They did not want to become Christians. The more the Jews remained true to Judaism, the harder the Christians tried to convert them. Often, the Christians were very cruel to the Jews. Sometimes the leaders of the Christian church led the converters. At other times the pope and the bishops protected the Jews.

Anti-Semitism means "hatred of Jews." People who hate Jews are called anti-Semites. In the next chapters you will follow the Ashkenazic Jews. Their story is one of anti-Semitism and the ways in which the Jewish community reacted to it.

Kneeling Jews reciting the Jew's Oath before a Christian judge in Augsburg, Germany, 1509.

chapter 14
The Jews of Germany

The story of the Jews of Germany is one with a beginning and an end. It ended with the greatest tragedy in the history of mankind. You may know some of the details of that tragedy. We call it the Holocaust. It resulted in the murder of six million Jews by Adolph Hitler and his followers. Hitler was the dictator of Germany. His followers were the Nazis.

This story started a long time ago. The first written record of the Jews in Germany goes back to the year 321 C.E., over sixteen hundred years ago. A well organized and large Jewish community existed in Germany. Most of Europe was ruled by Rome. The Christian religion had not taken over in that part of the world. The Jews in Germany enjoyed full civil liberty. They were free to live in the same way as their neighbors. They could earn their livings the same way their fellow citizens did. Some were farmers. Others were engaged in trade and industry.

This situation did not last very long. The Romans lost control. Christianity became the religion and way of life of Germany. More and more restrictions were placed on the Jews. At first Jews were allowed to continue to engage in business. The taxes they paid were higher than those paid by Christians. Gradually, more and more occupations were closed to them. There were only a few ways left for them to earn a living. One way was by lending money to Christian businessmen and charging interest for the use of the money. Today banks do the same thing.

In those days banking was not the honorable and respected profession that it is today. Christians could not charge interest. They were forbidden by church law. They thought that lending money and charging interest, as the Jewish money-lenders did, was wrong. Often they had no choice but to borrow the money they needed from Jews. The Jews were forced into this business. Other means of earning a living were closed to them. This situation did not make for happy and successful relations between Jews and Christians.

A Hebrew and German alphabet chart from 1477.

A page from a French history book written in 1337. The paintings shows the crusader attack on Jerusalem.

The Crusades

The Jews of Germany faced a greater problem. Many Christians believed it was their religious duty to convert people to Christianity. It was but a short step for ruthless leaders to convince their largely ignorant followers that all "non-believers" must be killed.

The year 1095 was almost one thousand years ago. The pope was the leader of all the Christians then. He organized the first "holy crusade." The crusade was a "holy war." The purpose was to drive the Moslems from the Holy Land (Israel). They wanted to rescue the tomb of Jesus, the founder of Christianity, from the hands of "non-believers." The crusader armies were organized for this purpose.

Bands of knights, soldiers, and monks assembled to march to the Holy Land. But many of them never got close to Jerusalem. On their way, they marched to the German cities along the Rhine River. They destroyed many Jewish homes and synagogues. They murdered thousands of innocent Jews.

Sometimes the priests and the bishops tried to save the Jews. But there was terrible destruction. The crusading armies made up reasons to justify their murdering of so many Jews. They said that the Jews desecrated Christian churches, that they were disloyal and committed treason, that they killed Christian children and used their blood to bake matzahs. They said that the Jews poisoned water wells so that Christians would get sick and die. Of course none of these things was true. But many of the Christians were uneducated and ignorant. They believed the stories and hated the Jews even more.

Costume of German Jews in the thirteenth century. Jews were required by law to wear pointed hats, so that everyone could know who they were.

The Ghetto

For hundreds of years the Jews of Germany lived in constant fear for their lives. There was always physical danger. And they were not permitted to mix freely with Christians. In every city the Jews were forced to live in a segregated section called the ghetto.

But in spite of all the hardships, life continued. The Jews established synagogues. They started schools. They developed a life entirely separate from the rest of the German community. They studied their Hebrew Bibles. They also studied other holy books. Many Jews became scholars. This was at a time when most Germans could not even read or write.

The Jews of the ghetto did not mix with other Germans. The German language they spoke soon mixed with many Hebrew words and expressions. Through

A medieval drawing of a Hebrew teacher and his young pupil (Germany, thirteenth century).

The Rashi Synagogue in the West German city of Worms. Rashi, the great scholar, worshipped here.

the years they developed a language of their own called Yiddish. It was a mixture of German and Hebrew. This language later spread to other parts of Europe. In each country more words were added to the Yiddish language. It is still spoken by some older members of Jewish families who have come to America from Europe. Many books, stories, poems, and songs are written in Yiddish. It is a language that can be heard in many parts of the world. It is a language that is in danger of dying out in America. This is unfortunate, because it means that an important part of the Jewish heritage may soon be lost to us.

Moses Mendelssohn and the Enlightenment

For many years the German Jews lived secluded in their ghettos. As modern times approached, things began to change. In the eighteenth century people began to realize that all human beings have certain rights. There was talk of freedom and equality. It was during this time, in 1776, that our own country was born. It was established on the right of all people to "life, liberty, and the pursuit of happiness."

This new spirit of equality spread. It went through most of Europe. It had an effect also on the Jews of Germany.

The synagogue in the Frankfurt ghetto.

Title page of the *Mishneh Torah* of Maimonides by Nathan Ben Simeon Halevi. Cologne, 1296.

Little by little some of them were permitted to leave the ghetto. A few even became well known among Germans for their accomplishments.

But most Jews in the ghetto were not ready to take their places in the "outside world." They no longer spoke the German language. They knew very little about the world outside the ghetto walls.

Moses Mendelssohn, cultural leader in Berlin in the eighteenth century, who wished to educate his fellow Jews so that they might be accepted as German citizens.

A German Jew named Moses Mendelssohn helped the German Jews to take their places in that outside world.

Moses Mendelssohn was an author and philosopher. He lived in Berlin. He was highly respected by the educated German community. He had left the ghetto as a young man. He moved freely about the "outside world." He was sure that soon his fellow Jews would be able to move about as he did. But he knew that they were not ready to leave the ghetto. They could not even speak the same language as other Germans. He wanted to help them learn German. Then they could take their place in the changing modern world. He thought about this for a long time. Soon he had an excellent idea. Since all Jews could read and understand the Hebrew Bible, he would translate the Bible into German. Then those Jews who wished to learn German could use the Hebrew Bible along with the German translation. That way they were able to teach themselves the German language. This was very important to them. They were being granted more and more privileges in Germany. Finally, in 1870, the Jews of Germany became full citizens of their country; now, they were equal in every way to other German citizens.

The old synagogue in Berlin.

The Holocaust

For a time the Jews of Germany prospered. They lived side by side with their neighbors. They enjoyed all the freedoms. They had all the opportunities

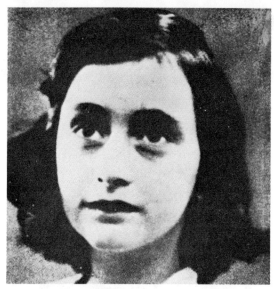

Anne Frank (1929-1945), teenage Dutch author of a diary describing the fear and desolate life of a young Jewish girl hiding from the Nazis in Amsterdam, Holland. She and her family were betrayed to the Germans and sent to a concentration camp, where she died.

enjoyed by other Germans. But this did not last for very long. In 1933 a cruel dictator came to power. He was named Adolph Hitler. He told the Germans that in order for Germany to prosper, only "true" Germans should be allowed to have the rights and privileges of citizens. Jews were not "true Germans," he told them. Of course he did not tell them that Jews had lived in Germany for over sixteen hundred years.

Many of the Germans believed Hitler. Times were bad in Germany. Many people did not have jobs. Often there was not enough food. It was easy to blame someone else for their troubles. Many of the German people welcomed Hitler's persecution of the Jews.

At first the German government just made things difficult for the Jews. It took away their businesses. It took away their money. It would not allow their children to go to German schools. And it took away their citizenship. But in 1939 Hitler and his government began to follow a new policy—the wholesale murder of the Jews. Millions of Jews—men, women, and children—were rounded up—often taken from their homes in the middle of the night. They were sent to concentration camps where they were put to death. Men, women, and children, whose only "crime" was that they were Jewish were put to death.

Hitler followed this policy of destruction in Germany and in all the countries conquered by Germany during World War II. Six million Jews were murdered by Hitler and the Nazis. This was the greatest tragedy that has ever happened to mankind. In many ways the world still has not recovered from the shock and horror. The events of this period are known as the Holocaust. They marked the end of the Jewish communities in Germany and in many other countries in Europe.

Distributing yellow Star of David armbands which, under the Nazi regime, Jews were forced to wear.

chapter 15

The Jews of Poland

The Holocaust was terrible. The Jews of Germany were completely destroyed. Judaism was completely wiped out in Poland also. At one time there had been a large Jewish community in Poland. It had been one of the most creative in the world. At the end of World War II there was hardly a Jew left in that country. Most had been murdered by Hitler. Some had fled to the United States or to Israel. They started new lives in their new countries.

Let us go back in history to the crusades. Many German Jews were killed. Many others fled from Germany and neighboring countries to escape the terrible consequences of the crusades. This was at the end of the eleventh century.

A Polish-Jewish fiddler by the Jewish artist Isidor Kaufmann.

Jews are known as the People of the Book. In this painting by Isidor Kaufmann, 1880, we see a Polish-Jewish scholar studying his holy books. Note the wool talit draped over the chair.

Many Jews moved to Poland. They were welcomed. They were treated kindly by the king and the Polish people. For many years the Jews lived happily and peacefully in Poland. They became merchants. They also became skilled laborers. They prospered. Poland was a land of farmers. It really needed the skills of the Jews in order to develop.

The Jews became more prosperous. They became content and secure. They were able to establish a highly developed and creative community life. Schools were established. They studied the Bible, Talmud, and other religious subjects. All Jewish boys attended school.

Stately house, in Lvov, of Simha Menahem, Jewish physician to John III Sobiesky (1624-1696), king of Poland.

A Polish-Jewish woman blessing the Sabbath candles. Notice how the house has been cleaned for welcoming the Sabbath. This painting is by Isidor Kaufmann.

They studied the great Jewish books. This was at a time when most Europeans could neither read nor write. Jewish girls did not attend school. They were taught by their mothers to read the prayerbook in Hebrew. They were also taught to read and write Yiddish.

In all Jewish homes the laws and rituals of Judaism were observed. The Sabbath was the most important day of the week. No one worked on this day. No cooking was done on this holy day. A special Sabbath delicacy called cholent was prepared before the Sabbath began. It was kept warm throughout Friday night. That way it could be eaten for the Sabbath afternoon meal without being reheated.

All Jewish holidays were observed. Jewish laws and customs were part of the everyday life of every Jew. Religious life flourished. The Jews were happy and contented.

Inside a Polish synagogue by Isidor Kaufmann. Notice the large library of holy books. The people are wearing fur hats. These hats are called shtreimlech. Chasidim wear these hats on holy and joyous occasions.

The Council of the Four Lands

The Polish king allowed the Jews to have a kind of self-government. The Jews of each city were permitted to elect representatives to a governing council called the Kahal. The original purpose of the Kahal was to collect taxes for the king. It soon became a Jewish self-government. It was concerned with all aspects of Jewish life.

Each Kahal collected taxes from its members. The money was used for Jewish schools, hospitals, rabbis and teachers. The Kahal appointed judges to decide civil disputes among the people. These disputes were settled according to Jewish law.

The highest Jewish governing body was the Council of the Four Lands. It was made up of representatives of the Kahals of the four large provinces of Poland. At this council matters were discussed which affected all the Jews of Poland. The men who attended the meetings of the council were the greatest scholars. They were the most re-

The meeting place of the Council of the Four Lands in Lublin in the sixteenth and seventeenth centuries.

spected Jews in all of Poland. The council helped to keep the Jews of Poland united. It was an important factor in keeping Jewish life strong and creative.

Page from the pinkas (minute-book) of the Council of the Four Lands, with signatures of delegates.

Troubled Times

Peace and prosperity did not last. In 1648 there was a revolt. The Cossacks fought against the Polish lords. The Cossacks hated the Jews because they had helped carry out the orders of the Polish government. Gangs of peasants and Cossacks caused terrible destruction. Hundreds of Jews were tortured and killed. Their property was destroyed.

The war continued for ten years. Peace was finally restored. The rich and

Bogdan Chmelnitzki, Cossack rebel leader responsible for the death of hundreds of thousands of Jews.

Model of a wooden synagogue in Poland.

A famous picture entitled "Golus," showing the bitterness of exile. Artist Samuel Hirszenberg shows Jews, young and old, forced to leave their homes in Russia by one of the many cruel decrees of the Czar.

powerful Jewish community had lost all its former glory. Many Jews had died. Many others had been injured or enslaved. Those who were left had lost their property. They were poor and desolate.

Many believed that the Jews of Poland would never recover from the terrible destruction. But slowly they began to reorganize their lives. They rebuilt their homes. The Council of the Four Lands was restored. Some measure of peace existed once more. But the Jewish community of Poland never again had the strength of earlier days.

In Hebrew cheder means "room." In Yiddish it was the name applied to Hebrew schools. Here we see students and a teacher in a Polish cheder studying Torah.

The Baal Shem Tov and Chasidism

Have you ever seen Jewish men with long beards and long sidecurls? They wear fur hats and long black coats. You must have wondered about these strange people who look so unusual. Their customs and clothing seem so odd. These people are called Chasidim. They belong to a movement that first started in Poland many years ago. The members of this group still dress as did their ancestors hundreds of years ago. The customs they observe are the same as those observed by their forefathers.

The Chasidic movement developed after the terrible revolt in Poland. The Jews of Poland were poor, unhappy, and discouraged. They needed comfort. They needed encouragement. The needed a leader who would give them new hope. Such a leader was Israel the Baal Shem Tov (Master of the Good Name).

Picture of a Polish Chasid by the Jewish artist Moritz Oppenheim. The background is the cover of a Torah Ark. The fur hat the Chasid is wearing is called a shtreimel. Many Chasidim wear such hats on holidays and happy occasions.

Israeli stamp with drawing of the synagogue of Rabbi Israel Baal Shem Tov. Most synagogues in the Polish villages were built of wood.

Israel was a kind and loving man. He believed that religion should be an expression of love for God. This does not seem like such a unique idea. But many of the people had forgotten the love and joy that can come from being a good Jew. They were concerned that all the laws of Judaism should be strictly obeyed. They forgot to feel the wonderful spirit and joy of being Jewish. Israel Baal Shem Tov taught the people to come close to God through prayer. But prayer alone was not enough. There must be singing with prayer. There must be dancing. And the people must be happy. Israel taught his followers to practice justice and charity. These, of course, are not new ideas in Jewish life.

A Hasidic Rabbi giving his blessings to a young follower, about 1815.

Girls learning Jewish law from a woman teacher.

But this great leader gave them new meaning and inspiration.

The Chasidic movement became very popular in Poland. Soon it spread to other parts of Europe. When the Baal Shem Tov died, his followers continued to follow his teachings. They continued to live their simple lives. They practiced generosity and charity. They observed their religion in joy and hope. Many of the descendants of the original Chasidim still wear the same clothing that was worn in Poland when the movement started. They worship in the same way as their forefathers. They still sing the lovely songs. They dance the dances that help to express their love for God and Judaism.

Chasidim dancing with joy at the Western Wall.

The Holocaust

The Jewish community continued to exist in Poland, but conditions were difficult. Those who were able to leave and go to the United States, or to the new Jewish settlements in Israel, did so. Many American and Israeli Jews are descended from Polish Jews. Perhaps you are descended from Polish Jews.

The end of the Polish Jewish community came during the time of Hitler.

After Germany conquered Poland in 1939, all the Jews were moved into ghettos. There were Jewish ghettos in Warsaw, Lublin, Vilna, and other cities in Poland. The ghettos were ringed by soldiers and the Jews were forced to stay there. They were very crowded. There was not enough food. The Germans hoped that most of the Jews would starve to death. Then they would not have to bother killing them in death camps.

Life was very hard for the Jews in the Nazi ghettos, but they did not lose hope

Leo Baeck was a German rabbi who refused to flee Germany. He was sent to a concentration camp where he continued to help the victims of the Nazis.

This famous photograph, taken from German archives, shows Nazi soldiers rounding up "the enemy" in the Warsaw ghetto. The last survivors, almost unarmed, held off a Nazi armored division for many days in the heroic battle of the Warsaw ghetto.

The Warsaw ghetto engulfed in flames.

or courage. There were art classes and music classes. There were lectures and plays. People continued to read and to learn. They tried to lead normal lives even in this terrible place. They did not die of starvation, disease, and despair as the Germans had hoped. So tens of thousands were sent to death camps to be killed.

At first the Jews in the ghettos did not know about the death camps. They thought that those who were being taken from the ghetto were going to work camps. They did not know that they were being sent to places where they would be killed. But soon they found out. In the Warsaw ghetto the Jews prepared to fight. They did not have weapons. They were able to steal or buy a few, and they made some in secret. They were still no match for the Germans. But they knew that they would die one way or the other. If they did not die fighting for freedom, they would die in the death camps.

They hoped the people of Poland would join the fight.

On April 19, 1943 the German soldiers marched into the ghetto. They were going to destroy it and kill all the Jews. They thought it would be easy because the Jews were half-starved and weak. But the Jews fought back. They shot at the German soldiers from windows and rooftops. The Jews fought hard. They would not give up. They fought for 28 days. Many German soldiers were killed and wounded. Finally the German air force bombed and destroyed the ghetto. Twenty thousand Jews were killed in the battle. But many Nazi soldiers died too.

The glorious Jewish community of Poland is no more. Just as Hitler and the Nazis totally destroyed the Jews of Germany, so too they destroyed the Polish Jewish community.

Mordecai Anielewicz helped organize the revolt against the Nazis in the Warsaw Ghetto. He died fighting the Germans. This statue in memory of Mordecai Anielewicz is at Kibbutz Yad Mordecai in Israel.

chapter 16

The Jews of Russia

This is the story of the Jews of Russia. It is both happy and sad. It is the story of one of the largest and most important Jewish communities in the world. It is a long story, a story of hope and creativity that is in danger of ending unhappily. You will read about the plight of today's Russian Jews later. But first let us start the story at the beginning.

It was the official policy of the Russian Czars to keep Jews and foreigners from settling in Russia. In 1772 the Russians swallowed up a large chunk of Polish territory. With the land, the Russians inherited about a million Jews. Whether they liked it or not, the Russians now had Jews in their land.

At first the Russians forced the Jews to live in a special area called the Pale of Settlement. Jews made their living as innkeepers, as skilled workers, and as wagon drivers. They were not allowed to live in other areas.

The Russian people and the Russian government were never friendly to the Jews. But the Russian Jewish community managed to survive and even to thrive. Jewish poets wrote poems in Yiddish and Hebrew. Jewish philosophers wrote books of philosophy. Jewish humorists and writers wrote novels and short stories. Jewish schools flourished. Jewish life in Russia was meaningful and intensely Jewish.

Jewish Education in Russia

Every boy received a Jewish education. It started when he was three or four years old. Every boy attended a cheder—a one-room school. There he studied Hebrew for many hours. From morning until evening the children learned to read and write Hebrew. They learned to translate the Bible into Yiddish. They memorized the prayers from the Hebrew prayerbook.

Students in Poland who have just started to study Hebrew wait their turn to recite. This painting is by the Jewish painter Moritz Oppenheim, about 1880.

At age thirteen the better students went to a higher school. It was called a yeshiva. There they learned more difficult Jewish subjects. They studied Bible Commentary, Midrash, and Talmud. When they finished this school they could be ordained as rabbis. Not everyone became a rabbi. Some became businessmen or laborers. But they too were often scholars of the Bible and the Talmud.

The Haskalah

Most Jewish boys went only to Jewish schools. They received only a Jewish education. But this changed in the second half of the nineteenth century. The Jews of Russia began to take an interest in the world around them. They studied subjects they had never learned before. They studied science, literature, grammar. They also studied philosophy and history. This period was called the Haskalah. Haskalah means "enlightenment." Many important and well-known authors, poets, and philosophers came from this people.

Shalom Aleichem

Shalom Rabinowitz was one of the best-loved writers of this time. He was known by his pen name, Shalom Aleichem.

Shalom Aleichem was an excellent storyteller and humorist. He was able to take even sad situations and write about them lightly and humorously. He wrote about the life of Jews in the small towns of Russia. His stories were filled with warmth and understanding. Even today his books are read.

Shalom Aleichem wrote in Yiddish. Many people called him the Jewish Mark Twain. Mark Twain is a famous American writer. Twain called himself the American Shalom Aleichem.

"Tevye the Dairyman" is Shalom Aleichem's most famous work. This is a group of stories about a poor dairyman who lived in a small village in Russia. Through Tevye we learn a great deal about the way Jews lived at that time. You may know something about Tevya yourself. He was the hero of the long-running Broadway musical, *Fiddler on the Roof.*

Chaim Nachman Bialik

Chaim Nachman Bialik was a poet. He was one of the greatest poets the Jews ever had. As a young boy he was a dreamer. He spent a great deal of

An Israeli stamp with picture of Shalom Aleichem.

Israeli stamp with picture of Chaim Nachman Bialik.

time by himself. He daydreamed about many things. He was fascinated by everything around him. He enjoyed walking in the fields. He liked exploring the forest.

When he was seven his father died. His mother had to support him and his seven brothers and sisters. They were very poor and unhappy. Many of Bialik's later poems tell about his sadness at this time.

When Chaim grew up he became a poet. He wrote poems in Hebrew. His poems were about the beauties of nature and about his own experiences. One of his most famous poems is called "Ha-Matmid" (The Scholar). It tells about the life of a yeshiva student. It is very beautiful and touching.

Chaim Nachman Bialik is called the Jewish national poet.

Ahad Ha-Am

Asher Ginzberg was another writer at this time. Like Shalom Aleichem he used a pen name. He called himself Ahad Ha-Am, which means "One of the People."

Ahad Ha-Am wrote scholarly and serious essays. He was concerned for the future of Judaism. He believed that Judaism could survive only if Israel became the Jewish spiritual center. He did not want Israel to be a political state. He wanted it to be a center of Jewish thought and culture.

Many people agreed with Ahad Ha-Am. Others did not. They believed it was more important for Israel to be a political state. Many years later Israel did become a political state. But it is a religious, spiritual, and cultural center too.

Ahad Ha-Am

Jewish Life in Modern Russia

The story of the Jews in Russia has a very sad ending. In the past there were good times and bad times. But Jewish life continued. Judaism managed somehow to remain strong.

In 1917 the Communists took over in Russia. Life became very difficult for Jews who wished to practice their religion. The Communist government was against any form of religion. Many synagogues were closed. The study of Hebrew was forbidden. Zionism was declared illegal. This had a very bad effect on Jewish life in Russia. To make matters worse, thousands of Russian Jews were killed by the Nazis during World War II. One place where many were murdered is Babi Yar, near the city of Kiev.

Years have passed now. Things have not gotten any better. Russian Jews may not publish prayerbooks or Bibles. There are no Jewish religious schools. There are very few rabbis or synagogues. Judaism is in danger of dying out in Russia.

Jews all over the world are very sad about the plight of the Jews in Russia. Many Jews in the United States have appealed to the Russian government. They have asked that Judaism be allowed to flourish. So far this has not helped very much.

chapter 17

The Jews in the United States

There are many Jews in Israel today. It is a Jewish country. The vast majority of the people who live there are Jews. But did you know that there are more Jews in the United States than in Israel? They make their homes in or around the large cities of our country. You will also find them in small towns and villages. They live in the East, South, Midwest, and Far West. They live in Hawaii and in Alaska too. There are Jews wherever you travel in this vast land of ours.

You have already read about the first Jews who settled here. They were Se-phardic Jews. They left Spain, Portugal, and South America to escape persecution. They came to the New World quite early in its history. You also read how these early Jewish settlers contributed to the growth of our country.

The Jews came to the United States in four "waves" of immigration. First came the Sephardic Jews, in the 1660s and 1700s. They settled in New York, New England, Philadelphia, and the South. They represented a very small percentage of the population. But they prospered. And they contributed greatly to the developing new country.

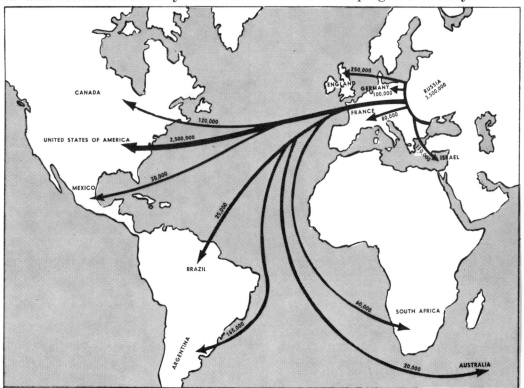

This map shows where Jews went from Eastern Europe between the years 1880 and 1934. The vast majority came to the United States.

The second wave was in 1820-1880. The Jews who came over during that time were from Germany. They came here in search of freedom and opportunity. Conditions were improving in Germany at that time, but the German government was not a democracy. And many German Jews wanted to live in a free country. The number of Jews in America increased during these years. In 1820 there were about 49,000 Jews in this country. By 1880 there were about 300,000. Many German Jews settled in the Midwest and the West. They helped to develop these areas of our country.

The third wave of immigrants came from Eastern Europe. They came from Russia, Poland, Hungary, and Rumania. Thousands of Jewish immigrants came between 1880 and 1924. They were escaping persecution and poverty in their homelands. Conditions were very difficult for them here. They managed not only to survive. They also made good lives for themselves and their families. Most of these immigrants remained poor all their lives. But most of their children went to college. Many of them became successful professionals and businessmen.

The fourth wave were those Jews fortunate enough to escape from Hitler. They came from Germany, Poland, Hungary, and other countries in Europe. Unfortunately only a very small minority of all the Jews who were af-fected managed to come to this country. The others perished.

Throughout the history of the United States, the Jews have contributed to the development of our country. In this chapter you will read about some of the contributions they made.

The Revolutionary War:
Haym Salomon

Most Jews supported the colonists in the Revolutionary War. Many made important contributions to the war. Haym Salomon was the best known. There are many ways to be a hero. Salomon was not a brave general. Nor did he give his life for his country. But he was a hero in the real sense of the word.

Haym Salomon was a very rich man. He lived in Philadelphia. Our government was very young and very poor. It needed money to pay its leaders and

This cartoon shows Uncle Sam welcoming immigrants from many countries. There was room for millions of newcomers and they were received with open arms. Between 1870 and 1920 thirteen million immigrants came to the United States.

soldiers. Often it did not have that money. Salomon gave money to the government to help pay the salaries of these men. He also lent money to several delegates to the Continental Congress. Their states were poor. Often these states did not send their delegates expense money on time.

Without the financial help of Haym Salomon, the colonists might never have won the Revolutionary War. Our country might never have been born. Included in the *Congressional Record* of 1850 is the statement that Haym Salomon was "one of the truest and most efficient friends of the country at a very critical period of its history." He was indeed that. All Jews can be proud of the part he played in winning the freedom we enjoy today.

Chicago's memorial to Haym Salomon, seen standing on one side of George Washington while Robert Morris stands on the other, both supporting him in his fight for freedom.

A bill of exchange obtained by Haym Salomon. At this time Benjamin Franklin was ambassador of the United States to France, a country that extended loans to America.

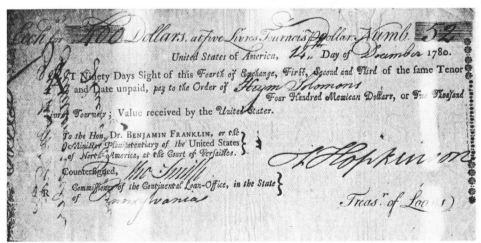

Isaac Mayer Wise

A New Way of Worship

The Jews flourished in the United States and the Jewish population grew larger. Soon there were Jewish communities in many parts of the United States. They built synagogues. They established businesses and prospered.

But Jewish life was different in the United States from what it had been in Europe. Here the Jews were equal members of their communities. They spoke English. They lived and worked side by side with their non-Jewish neighbors. Their children attended public schools as well as religious schools. They wanted their synagogues to reflect their new way of life. So many *reforms*, or changes, took place in Jewish worship. Prayers were recited in English as well as in Hebrew. Organ music was introduced. Some rabbis wrote their own prayerbooks. This was the beginning of Reform Judaism in the United States.

This movement grew until there are now over seven hundred Reform synagogues in this country.

A Great Rabbi: Isaac Mayer Wise

The man who was most responsible for the growth of this new Reform movement in the United States was Rabbi Isaac Mayer Wise.

Rabbi Wise came to this country from Europe. He became the rabbi of a congregation in Cincinnati, Ohio. He also started an English newspaper called the *Israelite*. He started a German newspaper for those who could not read English. He wrote a new prayerbook which he thought would be more meaningful to American Jews.

FIRST NUMBERS OF CURRENT JEWISH PERIODICALS.

Masthead of one of the early issues of the Israelite.

These accomplishments alone would have made Rabbi Wise an important and respected rabbi. But he did much more. He dreamed of organizing a union of congregations that would meet together and discuss common problems. He worked very hard for this goal. He was finally successful. The Union of American Hebrew Congregations was born. This organization is still in existence. Almost seven hundred American Reform congregations belong to it.

But even this was not enough for Rabbi Wise. He knew that if American Judaism was to grow, rabbis would have to be trained in the United States.

So Hebrew Union College, the first rabbinical school in the United States, was founded.

The campus of the Hebrew Union College in Cincinnati, which combined with the Jewish Institute of Religion in New York.

Many great rabbis were trained in this important rabbinical school. Now, cantors and educators for the Reform movement as well as rabbis are trained there.

In 1972 Hebrew Union College became the first rabbinical school to ordain a woman as a rabbi. Her name was Sally Priesand, and her first rabbinic position was as assistant rabbi at the Stephen Wise Free Synagogue in New York City.

Since then other women have been accepted as rabbinical students at the college. They are accepted on an equal basis with men and are trained to fill rabbinic positions in Reform congregations throughout the country. Women are also accepted as students in the Cantorial School of Hebrew Union College. A number of them have graduated and are now serving as cantors in Reform synagogues.

Rabbi Wise also organized the Central Conference of American Rabbis. It is an organization of rabbis. It now has almost a thousand members. Rabbi Isaac Mayer Wise was truly a great man. He

Front view of the "House of Living Judaism," national headquarters of Reform Judaism.

is an important part of the story of the Jews in the United States.

From Despair to Hope: The Immigrants from Eastern Europe

Many Jews had come to the United States from Germany between 1820 and 1880. But the largest wave was yet to come. In 1880 there were 300,000 Jews in the United States. By 1914 there were three million. They came from Russia, Poland, Rumania, and other countries. Most came to the United States to escape persecution and poverty. But what they found here was more poverty and a strange world whose language, customs, and way of life they did not understand.

In spite of all the hardships they endured, they found in this country one important thing that they did not have in their former homes—hope for the future. They were poor. They had to work desperately hard. But they knew that tomorrow would be better. The man who lived in an unheated, dark tenement on the Lower East Side of New York, and who worked long, hard hours in a sweatshop, always had hope. He knew that his son might become a doctor. And he knew his daughter could go to college. He could foresee a time when his children and his grandchildren would live good and happy lives as equal members of a free and democratic society.

This poster was published in 1917 during World War I. It appeals to the immigrants to purchase War Bonds.

Many of the best-known American Jews of our time are descended from these poor immigrants. Among them are

This 1919 painting by Maurycy Minkowski shows Eastern European Jews fleeing the pogroms.

The Statue of Liberty was presented to America by the French. This symbol of freedom in New York Harbor greeted the immigrants as they entered America.

political figures like Senator Jacob Javits of New York, Mayor Edward Koch of New York, and former Secretary of State Henry Kissinger. There are also business leaders like David Sarnoff, the late head of RCA, and Irving Shapiro, the president of Du Pont; medical researchers and scientists like Jonas Salk, who discovered a vaccine to prevent polio; Rosalyn Yalow, a Nobel Prize winner; entertainers like Sam Levenson, Danny Kaye, and Barbra Streisand; writers like Philip Roth, Saul Bellow, and Bernard Malamud; and many, many others. The children and grandchildren of the immigrants from Eastern Europe are found in virtually every field and occupation—music, art, literature, government, commerce, industry, science,

teaching. Most of them are not famous, but they live peaceful and comfortable lives. They live in a free and open society just as their immigrant parents and grandparents hoped they would.

Three Branches of Judaism

You read about Isaac Mayer Wise. He was the leader of the Reform movement. Many of the German Jews were members of Reform congregations. But the Jews who came from Eastern Europe were not interested in Reform Judaism. They were either Orthodox or non-believers. The Orthodox Jews formed many congregations in America. Their congregations had small synagogues. Their members all came from the same village in Europe. In this way they could keep some of their ties to the past in addition to observing their religion.

In 1888 the Orthodox Jews of New York tried to organize these small congregations into a unified Orthodox Jewish community. Rabbi Jacob Joseph of Vilna was brought to this country as chief rabbi. He tried to accomplish this task, but he found that it was not an easy job to accomplish. Finally, as the Orthodox Jews increased in number and became a more important part of the American Jewish scene, they too developed their own institutions. In 1896 a rabbinical seminary was opened in New York to train American Orthodox rabbis. It was originally called the Rabbi Isaac Elhanan Seminary and is now part of Yeshiva University. In 1898 the Union of Orthodox Jewish Congregations of America was founded to unite many of the Orthodox congregations in this country.

Reform Judaism met the needs of many Jews in the United States. Orthodox Judaism met the needs of many others. But there were some Jews who sought a middle ground. This need was met by the Conservative movement. Solomon Schechter, the famous scholar, became the head of the movement. As you read in an earlier unit, he was the man who discovered the lost book of Ben Sirach in the Cairo genizah.

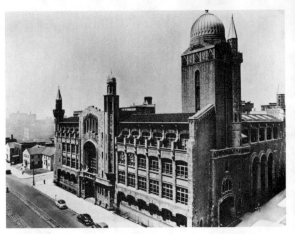

Yeshiva University in New York, Orthodox institution which includes high schools, undergraduate colleges for men and women, graduate and medical schools, and a rabbinical seminary.

The main campus of The Jewish Theological Seminary of America.

The three branches of Judaism flourished side by side. In our day many American Jews are affiliated with one or another of these movements. At first Reform Judaism served the needs of the German Jews. Orthodox and Conservative Judaism were popular among the East European Jews. Today we find Jews of both German and Eastern European ancestry in Reform, Conservative, and Orthodox congregations.

The American Jewish Community in Our Own Time

The Jewish community continued to grow in the United States. Today there are over five million Jews in our country. There are many congregations and Jewish schools. There are Jewish libraries and even Jewish museums. Jewish life has flourished. It has prospered in this country as in no other time and place in Jewish history.

There are Jews in all walks of life. Some are rich. Others are not. Some are businessmen. Others are laborers, professionals, or statesmen. At no time in history has a country been as good to the Jews as this one. All Jews have the opportunity to be successful and to make their contributions to society in any way they can.

The Jews have enjoyed wonderful opportunities in America. They have been able to do many things to help this country and make it proud of them. Jews have been military heroes and great scientists. They have been scholars and diplomats, inventors and government leaders. There have been Jewish mayors, Jewish congressmen, Jewish governors, and Jewish cabinet members. Perhaps someday there will even be a Jewish president.

UNIT V

A HOME IN ISRAEL

You have read about the early Jews. They used to live in the land we now call Israel. About four thousand years ago the Hebrew ancestors of the Jewish people wandered the country as nomads. They later became farmers and cultivated the land. It was in this land that the Jewish religion was born and the Bet Hamikdash, the Holy Temple, was built.

On two occasions in early history Jewish governments ruled Israel. But both times the land was conquered by enemies. First Israel was conquered by the Babylonians. That was in 586 B.C.E. Then the land was conquered by the Romans. That was in 70 C.E.

Even before this many Jews had lived in other countries. Many other Jews left the land afterwards. The Jewish community in Israel became smaller. The land was ruled by other peoples, first the Christians, then the Moslem Arabs, and after them the Turks. But some Jews always lived there. During the years when the Talmud was compiled, there were famous rabbis and scholars in the land. In the Middle Ages there was a large community in the town of Safed. There were always Jews living in the holy city of Jerusalem.

Most of the world's Jews, however, did not live in Israel. They lived in many other places—in the countries of Europe, North Africa, and the Middle East. Sometimes they were forced to move from one country to another. But wherever they went, they took their religious beliefs and customs with them. The Jews always hoped to regain Israel as a Jewish homeland.

In this unit you will read how the Jews made the dream come true. They did regain Israel as their homeland.

You may want to reread Chapters 5, 6, and 7. They will help you recall the early history of the Jews in Israel.

chapter 18

Zionism—If You Will It, It Is No Dream

For two thousand years the Jews were scattered throughout the world. But they could not forget Israel. It was their homeland. When they recited their prayers they turned eastward toward Jerusalem. Sometimes their prayers referred to Israel and the early days there. The Passover Seder service always ended with the words "Leshanah Habah Bi'rushalayim." These words mean, "May next year be in Jerusalem." Many Jews even bought small boxes of soil from Israel to put in their graves when they died. They wanted to feel that they were being buried in the soil of the Holy Land.

Yehuda Halevi was a great Spanish-Jewish poet. He lived about eight hundred years ago. He wrote beautiful Hebrew poems. It was his way of expressing his love for Israel. In one poem he wrote:

My heart longs for you from the far-off West.
If I could fly to you on the wings of eagles, I would soak your soil, with my tears.

For hundreds of years the dream of returning to Israel, or Zion, was just a dream. Many Jews prayed that some day a Messiah descended from King David would come. They hoped that he would gather the Jews from all corners of the world. And that he would bring them back to Israel, where they would live in peace and contentment forever.

Sir Moses Montefiore (1784–1885) was a British lord. He was a religious Jew and worked very hard to build up the land of Palestine. He built many hospitals, schools, and synagogues in Palestine.

But the miracle did not happen. It was not until the nineteenth century, when a number of dedicated men began to translate dreams into action, that the Zionist movement was born. It was this movement that eventually resulted in the establishment of the State of Israel.

Israeli stamp with picture of Baron Edmond de Rothschild (1854–1934). He helped build the modern State of Israel. He built farm settlements in Palestine and helped establish both the Hebrew University in Jerusalem and the Israeli wine industry.

Rabbi Yehuda Alkalai

Yehuda Alkalai was born in Serbia in 1798. He was the son of a rabbi. He spent his early life in Jerusalem. He too became a rabbi.

As a young man Yehuda became the rabbi of a congregation in Semlin, a town in Serbia. The Greeks were a neighboring nation. They fought and won a war of independence. In Serbia, revolutionary groups were preparing to try to gain independence from the Turkish government that ruled over them.

Yehuda Alkalai began to wonder if there was some way that the Jews could achieve freedom and independence. He wondered if Jews could have a land of their own. He wrote a book called *Shema Yisrael.* He suggested that it was not necessary to wait for a Messiah to perform miracles and take the Jews back to Israel. The Jews themselves could begin to establish Jewish colonies in the Holy Land.

This idea shocked many Jews. They believed that Israel would become a Jewish homeland only when the Messiah came. They thought that until then the Jews could only pray and wait. But some Jews agreed with Alkalai. They felt that only through their own efforts could the Jews bring about their dream.

Theodor Herzl
The Father of Modern Zionism

Theodor Herzl was an Austrian newspaper reporter. Young Herzl was a "liberated" Jew. He was not interested in Judaism. In 1894 Herzl was sent to Paris to report on the trial of Alfred

Bronze medal struck in honor of the second Zionist Congress at Basel. The quotation, from the Book of Ezekiel, tells of God's promise to bring the children of Israel from among the nations to their own land.

Dreyfus. Dreyfus was a young Jewish army captain. He was accused of selling French military secrets to the Germans.

Herzl sat through the trial. It became clear to him and to others that Dreyfus was innocent of any wrongdoing. His accusers were Jew-haters, or anti-Semites. They were persecuting the captain because he was Jewish. Herzl listened and watched. He became convinced that the Jews would never be safe and protected unless they had their own homeland. From that time on he dedicated his life to the establishment of a Jewish state in Israel.

Theodor Herzl

Herzl began his efforts to establish a Jewish state. He called a meeting of Jewish representatives from all over the world. This group was called the Zionist Congress. It began to plan for a Jewish state in Israel. This congress organized the Jewish National Fund to buy land in Israel. The land would belong to all Jewish people everywhere. Later it adopted a flag. That blue and white flag is now the official flag of Israel. It also adopted a national anthem, "Hatikvah" ("The Hope").

Soon Jews all over the world were working to establish a Jewish homeland in Israel. Young children were collecting pennies in Jewish National Fund boxes. They were helping to buy land for settlements. Who could have imagined in those days that fifty years after the first Zionist Congress the State of Israel would be born? Theodor Herzl was fond of saying, "If you will it, it is no dream." By his vision and zeal, he helped to make the dream a reality.

The Trial of Captain Dreyfus

chapter 19

Israel Becomes a Nation

Jews from all over the world worked to establish a Jewish homeland. They collected money. They interested world leaders in the idea. Others actually went to settle in the land. Israel, then, was governed by Turkey. But many young Jews established settlements on land bought by the Jewish National Fund.

Conditions were harsh and dangerous. The land had been neglected. Much of it was covered by swamps. Very little could grow there. Tropical diseases were widespread. The Arab neighbors of the Jewish settlers were often unfriendly, sometimes even hostile.

But the new settlers did not give up. They planted special trees to drain the swamps. They built houses and schools. They cultivated the land. Soon there were a number of flourishing colonies in the former wasteland.

Chaim Weizmann and the Balfour Declaration

Chaim Weizmann was a world-famous chemist. You may know him better as the first President of Israel. Strangely enough, these two roles are related. The story is fascinating and unusual.

When Chaim Weizmann was a young man, he taught chemistry at a university in England. Then came World War I. He became director of a chemical laboratory. He discovered a new method for making explosives. This helped the British to win the war. They were very grateful to this young Jewish scientist.

Because of his important contribution to the war effort, Dr. Weizmann had the opportunity to meet many important British leaders. He explained to them about Zionism and about the need of the Jewish people for a homeland. The British leaders were moved by what Weizmann told them. They agreed to do what they could to help Chaim Weizmann achieve his dream for his people. On November 2, 1917 the Balfour Declaration was issued. It announced that the British government was in favor of the establishment of a Jewish home in Palestine (Israel), and that it would help to establish this home.

Dr. Chaim Weizmann

Israel became an independent nation in 1948. Chaim Weizmann became its first President. This man had done so much to help in the establishment of the new nation. He was given the recognition and honor due him for his many years of work and service in the Jewish cause.

A Home at Last

You have learned about the Holocaust, the greatest disaster in the entire history of the Jewish people. When it was over, six million Jews had been brutally murdered. The vital and creative Jewish communities in Germany, Poland, Hungary, and other countries were completely wiped out.

The emblem of the modern State of Israel. The ancient seven-branched Temple Menorah is surrounded by olive branches. The olive branch is a symbol of peace.

David Ben-Gurion, first Prime Minister of Israel.

The world was shocked and horrified. The idea of a Jewish nation in Israel was gaining more and more popularity. On November 29, 1947 the General Assembly of the United Nations met to vote on whether there would be a Jewish state of Israel. Jews all over the world sat at their radios. They listened to the vote. At last it was over. More than two-thirds of the delegates had voted to establish a Jewish state. For the first time in two thousand years there would be a Jewish government in the land of Israel.

On May 15, 1948 the Proclamation of Statehood was read. Israel officially became a nation. The proclamation read in part: "By virtue of the historic right of the Jewish people and the decision of the United Nations, we hereby proclaim the establishment of the Jewish State, to be called the State of Israel."

The United States was the first nation to recognize the new state. Soon other countries followed. A new nation had been born. A Jewish state in the historic land of Israel was born.

Hostile Neighbors and Arab Aggression

The establishment of the State of Israel was not the happy ending that it seemed at first to be. As soon as the state was declared by the United Nations, the surrounding Arab nations attacked the new country. So life started for Israel with a cruel war. It brought death and hardship to the citizens of the nation.

Israel won the war. But the Israeli leaders realized that the Arab nations would continue to be hostile. They knew that the small new nation of Israel could exist only if it was always ready to defend itself against attack. And they were right. Three more times in the first twenty-five years of its life, Israel had to fight the Arab nations: the Sinai Campaign in 1956, the Six-Day War in 1967, and the Yom Kippur War in 1973.

An armed Israeli soldier praying at the Western Wall.

Israeli missiles on parade.

Fortunately Israel won each of these wars. But many people were killed or wounded.

In addition to the wars there are other dangers. Some Arab groups engage in terrorist activities. On many occasions small groups of hostile Arabs cross the borders into Israel. They attack Israeli soldiers who guard the frontier. Often they are captured by the Israeli soldiers before they can do any harm. But sometimes some of them are able to sneak into Israel. There they do much damage. Sometimes they bomb supermarkets, bus

Over eighty thousand people gather together for the memorial ceremony in Munich Stadium in honor of the thirteen Israeli sportsmen killed by Palestinian terrorists during the 1972 Olympics.

stations or other public places. Other times they attack and kill Israeli civilians—often helpless children.

In July 1972 a terrible thing happened. Israel sent a group of its star athletes to Munich, Germany, to compete in the Olympic Games. Arab terrorists broke into the hotel where the Israeli athletes were staying. Most of the athletes were killed.

Four years later, in June 1976, Arab terrorists hijacked a plane that belonged to France. The plane was on its way to France from Israel. Many Israelis were aboard. The terrorists forced the pilot to land in Entebbe, Uganda. When they landed there, the non-Israelis on the plane were allowed to leave and fly back to their homes. But all the Israelis were held prisoner. The Arabs made many demands from Israel in return for the safe return of the Israeli hostages. The Israeli government could not give in to these demands. Instead a group of Israeli commandos flew to Entebbe. They rescued all the Israeli hostages. It was a very courageous and skillful deed.

Another terrible terrorist attack took place on Saturday, March 11, 1978. It was called the Sabbath Massacre and was the worst terrorist attack in Israel's history.

On that day a busload of sixty three Israeli men, women, and children were on their way home to Haifa after an ex-

Israeli commandos on maneuvers somewhere in Israel. It was commandoes such as these who rescued the Israeli hostages in Entebbe.

American-born Yonathan Netanyahu led the Israeli commandos who rescued the hostages at Entebbe. He was the only Israeli soldier to be killed in the bold raid.

citing trip to some underground caves in Jerusalem. Everyone on the bus was in a happy, cheerful mood as they talked excitedly about the eerie beauty of the caves they had visited. Suddenly a group of armed terrorists on the side of the road began shooting at the bus. A little girl of five who was sitting on her father's lap was killed instantly. Her father was seriously wounded.

The terrorists continued shooting at the bus and at passing cars. By the time they were finally captured by the police, they had killed thirty five Israeli men, women, and children. Nine of the terrorists had themselves been killed, and one had been wounded. Two terrorists were captured by the police.

The Israelis would like to live in peace. But as long as there is danger, they know that they must be ready to defend themselves and their country. Every young man and woman is drafted into the army for several years after graduation from high school. Every person in Israel considers himself a soldier. In case of war or threat of war, people are called from their civilian jobs to defend their country. Even old people in their sixties and seventies serve in the civilian defense corps.

All Israelis, as well as Jews all over the world, hope that the Jews of Israel will finally be allowed to live in peace and contentment side-by-side with their Arab neighbors.

chapter 20

Modern Israel

Close your eyes and imagine what Israel is like. What do you see? Perhaps, because it is an old, old land—the land of the Bible—you imagine a country of old streets and ancient relics. Perhaps in your mind you see a very new country with modern buildings.

In either case you would be right. Israel is both old and new. It is the ancient land of the Bible. Archaeological artifacts can be found everywhere. It is also one of the world's newest countries. It has modern buildings and modern industries. It has brilliant scientists and the most up-to-date hospitals. And it has a democratic government.

This huge bronze Menorah is in the Knesset courtyard in Jerusalem. It was a gift from the people of England to Israel.

The people of Israel earn their livings in many different ways. Some are farmers. Others are policemen or government workers. Many work in factories or offices. Still others are doctors, scientists, musicians, artists, or any other occupation you can imagine. Some people live in kibbutzim. Others live in large cities,

Refugees from Arab countries on their way to freedom in Israel. In Israel they are welcomed with open arms. They are taught Hebrew and are resettled on farms, villages, and in cities.

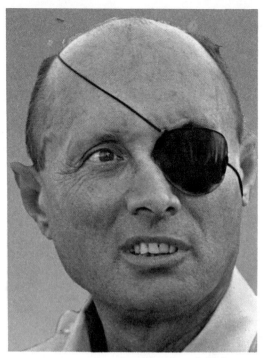

Golda Meir, first woman Prime Minister of Israel, 1969–74. As a young woman she was a Hebrew-school teacher in Milwaukee, Wisconsin.

Moshe Dayan, Israeli general and diplomat.

Israeli workers picking grapes for wine. Winemaking is a major industry in Israel. Israel produces many fine wines which are sold all over the world.

small towns, or villages. But whatever they do, or wherever they live, they love their country. They feel that they are "home."

The Government of Israel

Although the government of Israel is a democracy, it is different in many ways from the democratic government in our country. The government in Israel is called a parliamentary government, and it is like the government of Great Britain. Although Israel has a President, he is not the head of the government. His job is mostly ceremonial. The head of the government is the Prime Minister. But he is not elected directly by the people. Here is how the Israeli political system works.

Arab and Israeli Knesset members discussing a problem.

Voting in Israel

100

There are many political parties in Israel, not just two major ones as in our country. Each party stands for something different. Among them are the Labor Party, the Religious Party, the Socialist Party, and the Independent Liberal Party. Usually elections are held every four years. When an Israeli citizen votes, he votes for the party of his choice, not for a particular candidate. After the election, seats in the Knesset are given out according to the number of votes each party receives. The Knesset is the law-making body of Israel. It is something like our Congress, but even more like the French Parliament.

The party that wins the most votes chooses the Prime Minister. Usually he is the leader of the party. For almost thirty years the Israeli government was run by the Labor Party. David Ben-Gurion, Golda Meir, and Itzchak Rabin were Labor Party Prime Ministers. But in 1977, for the first time, another political party won the most votes. That party was Likud. Likud was formed in 1973 and is headed by Menachem Begin. When his party won the most seats in the Knesset, Begin became Prime Minister.

Begin has worked very hard to bring peace between Israel and her Arab neighbors. He surprised the world by inviting President Anwar Sadat of Egypt to visit Israel. And President Sadat came. He was greeted with great excitement and courtesy in Israel. Both Begin and Sadat expressed their hopes for peace.

Menachem Begin and Anwar Sadat meeting in Israel. Note the Arab plane in the background. Sadat flew to Israel in this plane.

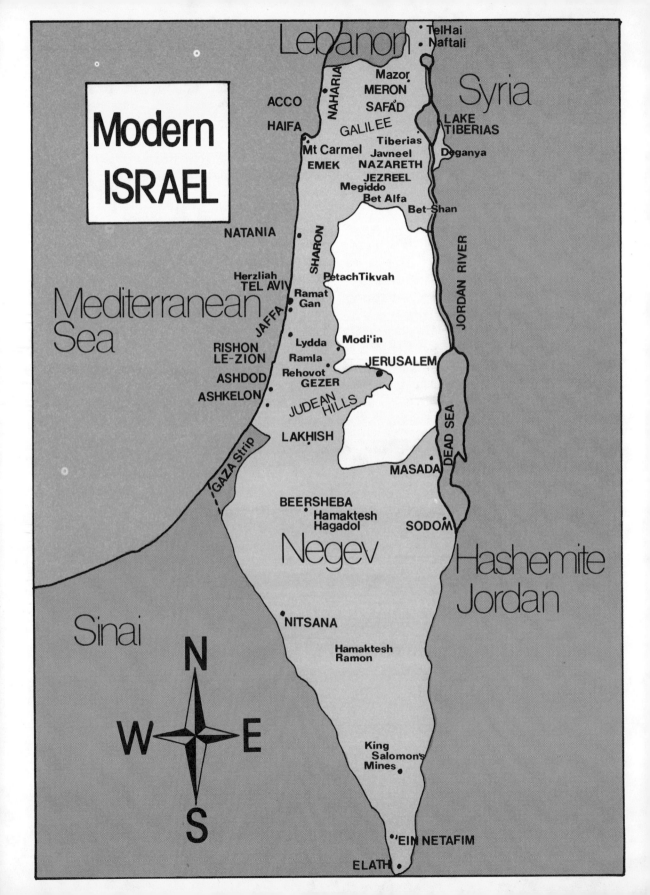

Highlights of Israeli History

Although Israel is a very young country, its short history has been filled with exciting, memorable, and sometimes sad events. Here are some of the highlights of that history:

1948: A new country is born. The State of Israel is proclaimed.

1949: Dr. Chaim Weizmann is elected President.
Israel is admitted to the United Nations.

1950: 110,000 Jews from Iraq are airlifted into Israel.

1952: Itzchak Ben-Zvi is elected President.

1954: Moshe Sharett becomes Prime Minister.

1957: The first ship arrives at the port of Eilat.

1958: The Beersheba-Eilat Highway is opened.

1960: The Bar-Kochba Letters are found in the Judean Desert.

1961: The trial of Adolph Eichmann opens in Jerusalem.

1963: Zalman Shazar is elected President.
Prime Minister Ben-Gurion resigns. Levi Eshkol becomes Prime Minister.

1965: The Israel Museum is opened in Jerusalem.

1966: The new Knesset building is opened in Jerusalem.
S.Y. Agnon receives the Nobel Prize for Literature.

An Israeli stamp showing part of the Israeli Declaration of Independence.

The Knesset building in Jerusalem, Israel. The Knesset is the legislative body in the State of Israel. There are one hundred and twenty members who are elected by a secret ballot.

1967: Israel is victorious in the Six Day War. Jerusalem is re-united.

1968: President Shazar is re-elected for a five year term.

1969: Golda Meir becomes Prime Minister.

1971: A new blood test for the early diagnosis of cancer is developed at Hebrew University-Haddasah Medical Center.

1972: A group of Israeli athletes go to Munich to participate in the Olympic Games. Eleven are murdered by Palestinian terrorists.

1973: Golda Meir is welcomed as a visitor at the Vatican.
Israel celebrates 25 years of independence.

1974: A Bedouin tribesman is elected as a member of the Knesset for the first time in Israel's history.

1976: Palestinian terrorists hijack a French plane with many Israelis aboard. The Israeli Army stages a successful heroic rescue at Entebbe, Uganda where the Israelis are being held hostage.

1977: Menachem Begin is elected Prime Minister.
Egyptian President Anwar Sadat visits Israel on a peace mission.

1978: Israel celebrates 30 years of independence.

Israeli jets defending the Land of Israel.

Israel is a democracy. Arabs and Jews have the same voting rights.

הכרזה על הקמת מדינת ישראל

DECLARATION OF INDEPENDENCE

OF THE

STATE OF ISRAEL

The Land of Israel was the birthplace of the Jewish people. Here their spiritual, religious and national identity was formed. Here they achieved independence and created a culture of national and universal significance. Here they wrote and gave the Bible to the world.

Exiled from Palestine, the Jewish people remained faithful to it in all the countries of their dispersion, never ceasing to pray and hope for their return and restoration of their national freedom.

Impelled by this historic association, Jews strove throughout the centuries to go back to the land of their fathers and regain statehood. In recent decades, they returned in their masses. They reclaimed a wilderness, revived their language, built cities and villages, and established a vigorous and evergrowing community, with its own economic and cultural life. They sought peace, yet were ever prepared to defend themselves. They brought blessings of progress to all inhabitants of the country.

In the year 1897 the first Zionist Congress, inspired by Theodor Herzl's vision of a Jewish State, proclaimed the right of the Jewish people to a national revival in their own country.

This right was acknowledged by the Balfour Declaration of November 2, 1917, and reaffirmed by the Mandate of the League of Nations, which gave explicit international recognition to the historic connection of the Jewish people with Palestine and their right to reconstitute their National Home.

The Nazi holocaust which engulfed millions of Jews in Europe proved anew the urgency of the reestablishment of the Jewish State, which would solve the problem of Jewish homelessness by opening the gates to all Jews and lifting the Jewish people to equality in the family of nations.

Survivors of the European catastrophe as well as Jews from other lands, claiming their right to a life of dignity, freedom and labor, and undeterred by hazards, hardships and obstacles, have tried unceasingly to enter Palestine.

In the second World War, the Jewish people in Palestine made a full contribution in the struggle of freedom-loving nations against the Nazi evil. The sacrifices of their soldiers and efforts of their workers gained them title to rank with the people who founded the United Nations. On November 29, 1947, the General Assembly of the United Nations adopted a resolution for reestablishment of an independent Jewish State in Palestine and called upon inhabitants of the country to take such steps as may be necessary on their part to put the plan into effect.

This recognition by the United Nations of the right of the Jewish people to establish their independent state may not be revoked. It is, moreover, the self-evident right of the Jewish people to be a nation, as all other nations, in its own sovereign state.

Accordingly we, the members of the National Council, representing the Jewish people in Palestine and the Zionist movement of the world, met together in solemn assembly by virtue of the natural and historic right of the Jewish people and of the resolution of the General Assembly of the United Nations, hereby proclaim the establishment of the Jewish State in Palestine, to be called Israel.

We hereby declare that as from the termination of the Mandate at midnight this night of the 14th to 15th of May, 1948, and until the setting up of duly elected bodies of the State in accordance with a Constitution to be drawn up by a Constituent Assembly not later than the first day of October, 1948, the present National Council shall act as the Provisional State Council, and its executive organ, the National Administration shall constitute the Provisional Government of the State of Israel.

The State of Israel will promote the development of the country for the benefit of all its inhabitants; will be based on precepts of liberty, justice and peace taught by the Hebrew prophets; will uphold the full social and political equality of all its citizens without distinction of race, creed or sex; will guarantee full freedom of conscience, worship, education and culture; will safeguard the sanctity and inviolability of shrines and holy places of all religions; and will dedicate itself to the principles of the Charter of the United Nations.

The State of Israel will be ready to cooperate with the organs and representatives of the United Nations in the implementation of the resolution of November 29, 1947, and will take steps to bring about an economic union over the whole of Palestine.

We appeal to the United Nations to assist the Jewish people in the building of its state and admit Israel into the family of nations.

In the midst of wanton aggression we call upon the Arab inhabitants of the State of Israel to return to the ways of peace and play their part in the development of the state, with full and equal citizenship and due representation in all its bodies and institutions, provisional or permanent.

We offer peace and amity to all neighboring states and their peoples, and invite them to cooperate with the independent Jewish nation for the common good of all. The State of Israel is ready to contribute its full share to the peaceful progress and reconstitution of the Middle East. Our call goes out to the Jewish people all over the world to rally to our side in the task of immigration and development, and to stand by us in the great struggle for the fulfillment of the dream of generations — the redemption of Israel.

With trust in Almighty God, we set our hands to this declaration at this session of the Provisional State Council in the city of Tel Aviv this Sabbath eve, the fifth day of Iyar, 5708, the fourteenth day of May, 1948.

INDEX